KT-102-745

THE PALM CENTRE
22 GUILDFORD ROAD
LONDON SW8 2BX
TEL (01) 720 8635

THE PALM SPECIALISTS

PALMS
FOR THE HOME AND GARDEN

PALMS
FOR THE HOME AND GARDEN

Lynette Stewart

ANGUS
& ROBERTSON
PUBLISHERS

Dedicated to all palm nuts.

ANGUS & ROBERTSON PUBLISHERS

Unit 4, Eden Park, 31 Waterloo Road,
North Ryde, NSW, Australia 2113, and
16 Golden Square, London W1R 4BN,
United Kingdom

First published in Australia
by Angus & Robertson Publishers in 1981
First published in the United Kingdom
by Angus & Robertson UK in 1984
Reprinted 1983, 1984, 1985, 1986, 1987

Copyright © Lynette Stewart, 1981

National Library of Australia
Cataloguing-in-publication data.
Stewart, Lynette.
   Palms for the home and garden.

   Includes index.

   ISBN 0 207 14270 X.

   1. Palms — Australia. 2. Palms — New Zealand.
   I. Title.

635.9' 345' 0994

Designed by Lynda Christie
Typeset in 10pt Tiffany Light by Setrite Typesetters
Printed in Singapore

Acknowledgements

I wish to thank all those in the palm industry who
freely gave their time and expert knowledge. My
particular thanks go to Bill Williams and Len
Dellow, both of whom are enthusiastic and
dedicated palm growers. I am grateful also to Del
Patterson for her inspired drawings and to Nicole
Lauricella for her time and interest in compiling and
editing the manuscript. Thanks also to my friends
Wendy Manning and Ray Bennett, without whose
enthusiasm and encouragement for this task I would
never have succeeded.

Illustrations by Del Patterson M.A.I.H.

The publishers acknowledge with thanks David and
Juliet Kimber of Arboreta Indoor Plant Hire for their
help and for the use of their plants and home for photography.

CONTENTS

PALM FASCINATION

1

In the mid-eighteenth century, palm collecting was an adventure for the intrepid botanist-explorer. George III was on the British throne and like other monarchs of his time patronised lavish botanical expeditions the like of which the world has not since seen. His friend Sir Joseph Banks was beneficiary of one such expedition when he voyaged to Australia with Captain Cook from 1768 to 1771. Banks's first botanical explorations on the Australian continent were led in the beautiful surrounds of a bay Cook named Botany Bay. His short expeditions would have carried him into dense stands of *Livistona australis,* a palm we call the cabbage tree palm. Some natural stands of this palm have survived along the eastern coast of Australia although most have disappeared due to the advancement of agriculture and suburban life.

Since those times palm collecting has been a popular hobby that has waxed and waned. During the nineteenth century indoor exotic plants soared to unprecedented heights of favour. Cacti, ferns, orchids and palms all took their turn at leading the lists of the most desirable acquisitions.

In the early nineteenth century Britain's nurseries numbered in the hundreds. A few became big businesses. One, owned by the Veitch family, was run by five generations and owed its success to the various family members who travelled all over the world in search of new exotics to reproduce back home for the insatiable British plant-seeking public. China, Japan, South America and the East Indies were searched by the plant hunters from Europe's nurseries. A great many of the plants were of tropical origin. Most plants died on the return sea voyage and the seed the travellers collected required special growing conditions for successful culture. The nurseries thus began developing better glasshouses to suit the requirements of their exclusive acquisitions. The botanic gardens of Europe competed with each other in acquiring the most elaborate hothouses,

monuments to the popularity of tropical plants. There followed important advancement in glasshouse heating techniques and equipment. Knowledge in plant breeding also took a leap forward as the nurseries laboured to produce their plants in big numbers. A plant enthusiast, Nathaniel Bagshaw Ward, developed glazed cases for carrying plants during long journeys. The idea came to him when he saw a fern grow in a sealed jar which contained some fresh earth. The fern thrived without added water or air. The "wardian cases", as they became known, were used to transport plants all over the world. They were the forerunner of the fashionable bottle gardens which were as favoured in Victorian parlours as they are today in our modern home interiors.

One botanist explorer who contributed immensely to increase our knowledge of palms was the German Carl Friedrich Philipp von Martius. In 1816 the Austrian King Max Joseph sent a scientific expedition to Brazil. Martius' reputation as a botanist of note influenced the king to include him in the company. They arrived in Rio de Janeiro in July on board the Austrian frigate *Austria.* With all preparations complete by December, Martius and his companion the zoologist Spix began the march through South America, searching and collecting, from the Tropic of Capricorn to the Amazon and its tributaries the Negro and Madeira. Along their way they collected 85 species of mammals, 350 birds, 130 amphibians, 116 fishes, 2700 insects and about 6500 kinds of plants. Usually several samples of each plant species were carefully preserved. Living plants and seed were placed under the care of the Munich botanical garden. The Munich herbarium's collection still conserves the preserved specimens. The explorations, which took almost three years, covered approximately 2600 kilometres. In spite of great difficulties which included even risks to life, the explorers were immensely successful in the volume and importance of their scientific results.

Martius wrote various works from his botanical studies. The most important is a huge three-volume work, *Historia naturalis palmarum,*, which took him from 1823 to 1853 to complete. He continued to gather palm specimens from all over the world and to work towards completing the most comprehensive study of palms that had ever been attempted. This publication has earned him the title for all time of "the Father of Palms".

Martius was fascinated by palms and is described as admiring them like a tourist, sketching them like a landscape painter and studying them like a botanist. Martius wrote of himself: *"In palmis semper parens juventus; in palmis resurgo"* ("In palms ever appearing youthful; in palms I am revived").

Indeed it is not difficult to understand why people become enamoured of palms. Their luxuriant foliage lends them a certain botanically primitive character which is not equalled among other plant families. As potted plants they are unsurpassable in an interior décor. As street, park and garden trees they may be either complementing or dominating but they always are an enrichment to any landscape.

The following chapters are written with the aim of providing readers with a basic understanding of these wonderful plants by dispelling some of the mystique which surrounds their culture and their maintenance inside the home. The use of botanical names is unfortunately unavoidable in any description of palms because of the various and changing common names that have been and continue to be used. The only way two people can be sure they are talking about the same palm is to identify it by its Latin name.

Readers who are interested in furthering their study of palms past the preliminaries provided by this book could find no better recommendation than to join the Palm Society. It is an international non-profit organisation engaged in the study of palms and the dissemination of information about them. Everyone interested in palms is eligible for membership and the Society boasts worldwide membership which includes palm nurserymen and botanists but mostly palm hobbyists. Their excellent quarterly journal, *Principes,* is devoted to information about palms. The address of the Palm Society is Box 368, Lawrence, Kansas 66044, U.S.A.

PALM BOTANY

2

Sometimes friends ask me to identify a palm they have growing in their garden. Without seeing the plant I must rely on their verbal description which usually goes like this: "You know, it is like a normal palm, tall trunk and spreading leaves on top". This of course proves only one thing, that people recognise palms as palms without much trouble. However, their powers of observation do little to help me identify the palm.

Palms are indeed a distinctive family. But not all palms are so easily identified as such and conversely not all plants supposed to be palms are true palms. The Palmae family, which includes 2500 or more species, most of which are tropical, belongs to the botanical subclass of flowering plants called Monocotyledonae. This makes them quite different from most ornamental plants, shrubs and trees.

Generally a palm consists of a single stem or trunk, a crown of leaves and a root system. New roots develop from the base of the trunk while all new leaves develop at the top of the trunk, from a point called an "apical bud".

Hearts of palms

The apical bud of numerous species of palms is the delight of the gastronome. But it is an unfortunate choice, for when the tender bud or "heart" is removed, the palm, if the stem is solitary, dies. Such destruction for the sole purpose of savouring the delicate taste and texture of palm hearts has been a major factor in the almost complete elimination of wild palms on Mauritius. Other palms undergo similar threat in different parts of the world. The early settlers of Australia supplemented their meagre rations with the hearts of the cabbage tree palm (*Livistona australis*) which grew then in abundance along the eastern coast. But more than the

search for fresh edible vegetation, the land clearing due to expansion of agriculture decimated this beautiful endemic plant.

Root system

The palm has a fibrous root system: the roots, developing from the same point at the base of the trunk, are all of fairly uniform size. This contrasts with trees and shrubs which have a tap root system: secondary rootlets branch from a central main root. As roots die off, new ones emerge and branching is infrequent. The root mass or "rootball" of a palm can occupy a small space if the soil supplies plenty of nutrients. This explains why large palms can miraculously thrive in small pots.

Palms do not produce those monstrous devastating roots, the scourge of garden pipes, fences, walls and septic tanks. It is quite safe to plant a palm within a metre or so of the house or wall. The roots will develop within a fairly small area although they may penetrate the ground quite deeply.

The trunk

You may have noticed that a young palm will, for several years, produce many leaves without developing a trunk. Unlike most plants, which increase in height and girth simultaneously, palms increase in girth before growing in height. When finally the trunk does start to grow in height, it has already reached its final width. In the life of a palm, the width of the trunk is thus determined at an early stage. This width does not normally vary from top to bottom. Of course there are exceptions and these are characteristic of the particular palm species. The trunk of the spindle palm (*Hyophorbe verschaffeltii*), for example, has the shape of a bottle, bulbous in the main body and tapering towards the top.

While the age of felled trees can be estimated by counting what are called the growth rings, this is not true of palms as they do not have them. Nor do they produce bark. The water- and food-conducting tissue (xylem and phloem), rather than being in the outer rim, is actually all through the trunk. The supportive wood is extended up and down the trunk like reinforcing rods in a concrete pylon. It is that structure which gives palm trees their wonderful flexibility and strength when faced with strong wind conditions.

Although the majority of palms are single stemmed, many produce offshoots from the base which develop into new stems. These offshoots, called "suckers", can be removed and grown independently into a new plant. Palms with a suckering habit will often develop clusters of stems. They are clustering or multistemmed palms.

While a few palms have underground trunks, others have trunks creeping across the ground. Yet another group clings as a vine to the branches of trees in rainforests.

Leaves

The number of leaves on an adult palm at any one time is fixed within a very narrow limit and is set for each particular species. As an old leaf dies and falls, a new leaf is developing within the crown. It is this continual process of leaf replacement which ensures the growth in height of the palm.

The part of the leaf which clasps the trunk is called the leaf base. Some palms have sheathing leaf bases which expand and wrap around the new ascending leaf bud. Many leaf bases can actually wrap one inside another around the innermost leaf bud. The result, called "crownshaft", is a swollen extension at the top of the trunk.

Costapalmate leaf

Pinnate leaf

Bipinnate leaf

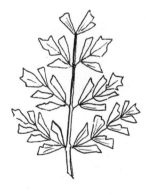

Palmate leaf

Flowers

Palm flowers and fruits are borne on stalks appearing amongst the leaves in some species, below the leaves in others. The flower stalk, called a "spadix", may or may not be branched. A sheath called a "spathe" protects the spadix before it emerges.

Sexual characteristics vary a great deal from one species to another. In some species each flower possesses both male and female organs (hermaphrodite). But in many palms male and female flowers are separate, borne sometimes on the same plant (monoecious), sometimes on different plants (dioecious). In dioecious palms pollen must be carried from male flowers on one plant to female flowers on another plant by insects or wind.

In some cases, like that of the talipot palm (*Corypha*), the tree flowers only once in a huge 8 metre high inflorescence containing about 60 million blossoms. After the fruit has ripened the tree dies.

The scars and rings seen on some palm trunks are the old bases left after the leaves have fallen. Phoenix palms present a distinctive diamond pattern of old leaf bases. Some palm leaves stay attached to the trunk long after they have died. The trunk of the American cotton palm (*Washingtonia robusta*) is sometimes covered with a "petticoat" of old dead leaves.

Leaf types

Palms show a variety of leaf types. The most common are the fan leaf or palmate leaf, the feather leaf or pinnate leaf and the so-called costapalmate leaf. The pinnate leaf shows a variation called bipinnate or fishtail. Usually the first leaves produced by seedling palms are simple grass-like leaves. A few palm species produce juvenile leaves which copy their adult form.

Fruits

Palm fruits normally hold only one seed but in a few species they hold two or three. Fruits are usually more decorative than flowers and some give a brightly coloured display. Bangalow palms (*Archontophoenix cunninghamiana*), native to the east coast of Australia, display in summer a beautiful shower of bright red fruits.

Fruits and seeds vary in size and colour from one species to another. In some palms the fruit is fleshy and edible when ripe. The date palm and the coconut palm, for example, provide an important source of food. The largest fruit in the plant kingdom is that of the coco-de-mer (*Lodoicea*) which can weigh 20 kilograms and is so dense it will not float. Some seeds like those of the palm vines *Calamus* are beautifully patterned like snake skin.

PALMS AS INDOOR PLANTS
3

Palms are once again in fashion. They are the stock-in-trade of the interior decorator and a delight to the indoor gardener. Today's houses and flats have airy, brightly lit rooms often open in aspect to gardens and views. Architectural fashions of the past dictated closed dark rooms, small windows, heavy curtains and a consequent reliance on artificial lighting. In contrast, modern interiors offer conditions more conducive for growing plants. And luxurious foliage placed against the stark angular contours of the modern room softens its harsh lines while giving it that fresh touch of "nature".

Using plants in a specific way, the interior decorator can create a subtle or dramatic effect. Artistically placed, potted palms, used alone or in groups, can be a striking feature in decoration.

Unfortunately interior decorators rarely care for the welfare of the potted plants they are using. For them the plant is a tool, solely for the purpose of highlighting a particular décor even if it means placing it in an unsuitable environment. But the potted plant is a living, growing thing with special needs and sensitivities to its environment. Home gardeners do or at least should care for the welfare of their plants. Lack of care will certainly cost them a lot in replacement plants.

Providing a home for your palms

Apart from the question of décor, you should consider the light, warmth and humidity that your plant needs. As a general rule most palms, if they are to be grown indoors, do best under bright rather than dull light, relative warmth rather than cold and a humid rather than dry atmosphere. Only a few palms will tolerate poor light but fortunately many palms will survive, though not thrive, in the commonly cool and dry atmosphere indoors.

The optimal climate is costly to arrange. Heating for conservatory conditions is expensive to install. The real enthusiast will sometimes stand the expense but the majority of people prefer to battle on with the means at their disposal. However, choosing the plant and determining its position requires some forethought. You should at least protect the plant from the shock of wide temperature changes, guard it against draughts and provide it with a minimum of humidity. Groups of plants will maintain their own slightly humid environment. Misting plants with water can be a tiresome method as it needs to be done several times each day. Some methods of providing a humid atmosphere are discussed in chapter 4.

Less expensive alternatives to a conservatory can be envisaged. While hobby glasshouses are becoming more and more popular in Australia, the use of shadehouses is already very widespread. A sunroom that catches winter and summer sun is often a good substitute conservatory. If part of its ceiling is glass, then the level of light is greatly improved. Be wary, however, of exposing your palms to direct sunlight. The leaves may easily burn, giving way to brown patches when the tissues die. Palms prefer brightly lit positions protected from direct sunlight. Glass presents also the advantage of heating the room. On a sunny day the sunroom can not only serve as a substitute conservatory but as a room for relaxation and entertainment.

Palms for their ornamental qualities

Several criteria should be considered before selecting a palm for its decorative qualities. Palms offer a great variety of foliage. The pinnate or feather leaf and the fan leaf are most common. Some indoor palms have fishtail leaves. (See chapter 2 for a fuller description of leaf types.)

Some palm leaves are quite delicate. The parlour palm, for example, has a neat little feather-type leaf. These palms grown indoors remain relatively small, usually under

Potted palms come in various shapes and sizes.

a metre in height. To obtain a leafy and bushy appearance, clump several plants together. A much bolder foliage is that of the golden cane palm, which is of the same feather type but much larger and stronger, its leaves curving and twisting in an interesting fashion. Golden canes form suckers and eventually grow into bushy plants with multiple stems. A large tub of bushy golden cane palms looks quite dramatic by glass or water. Similarly the Kentia (*Howea*) palms show bold dark glossy green foliage. Restaurants and offices often favour these decorative palms. They are well suited to indoor light conditions and display a classically beautiful foliage.

In contrast the shining dark green fingers of the *Rhapis* palms look quite exotic. Leaves are of the fan type, the divisions of which, called leaflets, are finger-like and droop attractively. The stems are fine and bamboo-like. Several stems in the same pot can be beautiful. The wide luxurious fan leaves of the Chinese fan palm look different again. These large but softly weeping leaves are particularly attractive indoors. The unusual fishtail leaflets of palms such as those belonging to the genus *Caryota* quickly catch the eye of even the casual observer. The segments or leaflets look as if they had been clipped with pinking shears. Each leaflet appears jaggedly edged but the whole leaf is quite perfectly regular in the arrangement of its com-

posite segments. A *Caryota* palm will give your room the touch of a palm collector.

The size and spread of the palm is another delicate point to consider. This criterion should definitely influence your choice of specimen. Palms can be kept quite small indoors for many years. When choosing a small potted palm do not expect it to double its size in a year as you may expect from other plants. If you wish to encourage new growth, give the palm a couple of months' summer vacation in a protected shady spot outdoors. Considering the slow growth of palms it is advisable to choose your palm at or close to the size you ultimately wish for it. Remember that, grown indoors, a Kentia seedling may take five to seven years to reach just a metre in height.

If you desire a low spreading fine-leaved palm, the dwarf date palm is a good choice. This palm, like the fan-leaved palms, seems to require more horizontal than vertical space. Advanced Kentia palms make splendid tall specimens, as do golden cane palms. Be sure of the dimensions of your chosen location or you may regret an impulsive purchase.

Inspect the plant before you purchase

What do you look for in a potted palm? First of all you want luxuriant, uniform-

A delightful grouping of, from left to right, *Chamaedorea elegans*, the parlour palm, *Arecastrum romanzoffianum*, the Cocos palm, and *Chrysalidocarpus lutescens*, the golden cane palm.

A profusely-flowering crab cactus is combined with *Phoenix roebelenii*, the dwarf date palm, for a stunning effect.

ly coloured, undamaged foliage which indicates the plant is healthy. Leaves should not be mottled, with fading or brown tips. Similarly, dead spots scarring the leaves can indicate previous damage, perhaps from direct exposure to the sun or frost. While browning leaf tips may be natural in the older lower leaves, the newer leaves should not show this kind of damage. In such a case, overwatering, overfertilising or even a pest-infested root system may be the problem.

Check the plant carefully for obvious signs of pests and disease. Yellow or brown flecks on leaves may indicate presence of scale or mealy bug. Inspect the underside of the leaves for these pests. Similarly, red spidermite, harder to detect with the naked eye, will leave a general pin-point yellow dotting of the affected leaves. If the plant shows only little damage from pests, it may still be a good purchase. Lightly sponging the plant with water and cotton wool will clean it up and a chemical spray should rid the plant of the offending insects. Regular spraying every few weeks for a couple of months may be necessary.

A general overall yellowing of the plant may indicate a need for fertiliser or trace elements. Another cause can be too much exposure to sun. Indeed, in response to too much light, the leaves start to lose their green pigment or chlorophyll.

Acclimatising your palm

Once your palm is home, it is not a bad idea to do a little cleaning operation. Either sponge the leaves or hose them gently with water. This will refresh the plant and remove more transient insects as well as washing off any pesticide residues which may be clinging to the foliage. It is advisable to soak the soil. Allow it to drain and give it another soaking. This will wash out most mineral salts accumulated in the potting soil. Check the undersides of the leaves thoroughly for insect pests. If you notice or suspect the presence of some insect, spray with an appropriate insecticide such as Malathion.

Next step is to pick a nice shady spot on a patio, terrace or veranda. A shadehouse is very suitable if you are lucky enough to have one. This spot will serve as a "half-way house" for the palm before it is brought indoors to a darker place. If you know for certain that the palm has been grown under shadehouse conditions and has not been subjected to bright sunshine, then you can forego this half-way step. You should detect no change in the plant and the foliage should remain fresh and healthy. Leave the palm for about two weeks in its half-way house, hosing down or misting the foliage twice daily. If the weather is hot the palm will of course need to be watered at the roots. Do not allow the soil to dry out.

Repotting may also be necessary if the container is too small and roots are growing out of the drainage holes. Check this by removing the plant from the pot. The best way to do it (for small palms at least) is by upturning the pot while supporting the plant's base and the surrounding soil with one hand whilst lifting the pot from the root mass with the other. A mass of roots with little visible soil indicates that repotting is necessary. For repotting procedures see chapter 4.

After a fortnight in the half-way house the palm is now ready for a trial indoors. Any location which provides plenty of bright but indirect light should be suitable. If the position you have chosen for its permanent location is brightly lit, you can place the palm there straight away. It may adjust without further steps. Remember, however, that at only approximatively one metre from the window the light level drops remarkably. While your eyes adjust quickly, the palm may need progressive adjustment to this drop in light.

Once acclimatised to its indoor position, the palm will still only grow very slowly. To encourage new growth it is advisable, as I have previously suggested, to take the palm outside in summer to a shaded protected position. Within a few weeks this will bring on fresh growth and revitalise the foliage. It is a common misbelief that taking plants outside into the sun is good for them. A few hours or even less of sunbathing will most probably cause irreparable scorching to the foliage. Some palms will withstand this treatment better than others, though delicately leaved palms will certainly not take this type of mistreatment.

Location and arrangement

The foliage of palms can be used as the main element to create a stunning yet simple decorative effect. First of all the scale of the location must be assessed. A tall large-leaved Alexandra palm would not suit a small bathroom for example. Similarly a small parlour palm would be made insignificant in the corner of a large boldly decorated living room. In general large-leaved palms succeed in softening the harsh contours of modern rooms. Smaller delicately leaved palms look well as a focal point in a small room.

The luxury of dense foliage provided by massed plants — particularly if of the same kind—can create a strong impact. Planter boxes massed with foliage plants can be used to divide a room or fill an architecturally awkward space. Best associated with palms are plants whose foliage does not compete. The small leaves of *Peperomia*, the cascading foliage of ivy and the dainty shiny dark leaves of the weeping fig are compatible. Even the *Fatsia* or *Monstera deliciosa,* which have large uneven-shaped leaves, are good neighbours for larger feather-leaved palms. The spiky foliage of some dracaenas and cordylines tend to compete with the foliage of palms and should be avoided.

In offices plants are more likely to suffer from their environment. Lighting and air-conditioning will probably be turned off at weekends. The air of offices is often too dry and plants are likely to be neglected by the office occupants. Many companies now hire large plants and have them looked after by contract firms. The plant that starts to deteriorate is replaced before it becomes an embarrassment. But the less extravagant amongst us will rather choose small hardy plants to adorn the office desk or window sills. Planter boxes filled with small foliage plants are fairly easy to maintain. When selecting a palm for an office, you should also be careful to choose from the hardier species which are suited to low light intensities. For such conditions, the dwarf date palm and the Kentia palms are good choices. With its spread of softly weeping leaves, the dwarf date can give interest and beauty to the dullest corner. As for the Kentia palms, they look well either alone or in groups. Their foliage is particularly enhanced against a blank office wall which they in turn enliven.

Containers

Although the focus should be kept on the plant rather than the pot, the aesthetic function of the container nonetheless cannot be ignored. Pure shapes and plain colours harmonise best with the dominant foliage of palms. Glazed earthenware pots in subdued colours, copper or brass buckets or tubs, and plain or pastel-coloured plastic containers are usually good choices. Terracotta pots, which are simple, natural and earthy in colour and texture, are also suitable.

An important criterion to consider before selecting a container for your palm is the material of which it is made. Plastic is non-porous and fragile. Flexible pots made from polyethylene are more sturdy. More expensive terracotta is easily broken but porous so excessive water and salts are more easily leached out into the clay. Polyethylene bags are cheap and useful, light and fairly easy to handle, but they are no permanent home for an indoor plant, so repotting will be necessary.

Key to ratings:

 Most suitable.

 Usually suitable given good location and care.

Less suitable; short periods indoors only as requires high light levels.

Palms suitable for indoor conditions

PALM	COMMON NAME	SUITABILITY
Archontophoenix alexandrae	Alexandra palm	🌴
Archontophoenix cunninghamiana	Bangalow palm	🌴
Arecastrum romanzoffianum	Cocos palm	🌴🌴
Caryota mitis and *C. urens*	Fishtail palm	🌴🌴
Chamaedorea elegans	Neanthe bella Parlour palm	🌴🌴🌴
Chamaedorea erumpens	Bamboo palm	🌴🌴🌴
Chamaerops humilis	European or Mediterranean fan palm	🌴
Chrysalidocarpus lutescens	Golden cane palm	🌴🌴🌴
Howea forsteriana and *H. belmoreana*	Thatch palm, Kentia palm	🌴🌴🌴
Laccospadix australasica	No common name	🌴🌴🌴
Linospadix monostachya	Walking-stick palm	🌴🌴
Livistona australis	Cabbage tree palm	🌴
Livistona chinensis	Chinese fan palm	🌴🌴
Phoenix canariensis	Canary Island date palm	🌴
Phoenix roebelenii	Dwarf or miniature date palm	🌴🌴🌴
Ptychosperma elegans	Solitaire palm	🌴
Rhapis humilis and *R. excelsa*	Lady palm	🌴🌴🌴
Trachycarpus fortunei	Windmill palm	🌴

Palms suitable for indoor conditions

The table on page 11 shows the suitability of some common palms to indoor conditions, i.e. their ability to adapt to low light intensities and survive in a fairly dry, unheated environment. See also the more detailed comments on each palm in chapter 7.

Palms unsuitable for indoors

There are some species of palm often sold as suitable for indoor use but which should be restricted to open or semi-shade positions in the garden. These are *Butia capitata* the Wine palm, *Roystonea regia,* the Royal palm and the two American cotton palms, *Washingtonia robusta* and *W. filifera.* All need higher light intensities than can be obtained indoors.

THE CARE OF POTTED PALMS
4

Palms are generally quite hardy for indoor conditions. They will withstand mistreatment better than many other plants used indoors. Nevertheless neglect or "overcare" can damage them irremediably. Palms usually grow slowly indoors and this calls for a light hand with the water and fertiliser. Overfertilising and over-watering are common mistakes. Less frequently, perhaps, a neglected palm will die of thirst. Cold draughts or wide temperature fluctuations may also take their toll. Insect pests can cause leaf damage which spoils the appearance of the plant.

Rotate your palms

To take the guesswork out of growing palms indoors, it is advisable to give each plant a chance to refresh its growth outdoors. I prefer not to subject my palms to just a few short hours outside, in the rain or under a shaded tree. My potted palms live in rotation between indoors and my shadehouse. A wind-protected courtyard or patio will substitute for a shadehouse provided that plants are not exposed to direct sunlight. One month inside and two months outside seems to me a good rotation plan for the faster growing tropical and subtropical palms. The hardier, slower growers can stay inside longer without any visible damage.

Apart from establishing a plan of rotation for your palms, it is important to know about the conditions which will best suit them indoors. The wide variety of palms and their natural habitats makes it hard to set down specific rules for growing palms indoors. Nevertheless some general guidelines can be drawn.

Requirements for growth

Plants need light, water, air and minerals for growth. A seed stores within itself the nutrients for the germination and growth of the young seedling. But the stores of the seed are quickly depleted and to assure its growth the plant must then depend on its environment. Each plant species has an optimum environment. How close we come to discovering and re-creating that environment determines just how well the plant will grow.

A white or pastel colour wall will increase the reflected light.

Some palms have narrow environmental limits to their growth and are therefore more exacting to grow, but many palms develop in a wide range of environments. These hardier palms are of course much easier to grow successfully.

Light: The light available to a potted palm is the most critical and limiting factor to its successful growth. Indoors, palms need filtered or indirect bright light. With less light growth will slow down and perhaps almost stop. A palm that does not receive sufficient light to grow will eventually die, although this may take several months. It is therefore difficult to quickly determine if a palm is

	NATURAL LIGHT CONDITION	DESCRIPTION
Preferred	Filtered bright light	Direct sunlight filtered by a fine curtain or blind or by foliage outside the window.
	Indirect bright light	Close to an area where direct sunlight falls.
Usually suitable	Indirect medium light	Close to a window receiving bright indirect light. Best windows for catching light face north, north-west or north-east. May be only 10% of the light intensity of direct sunlight.
Unsuitable	Dim light	Two metres or more from a light source; corners receiving little light; dimly lit rooms. May be only 5% of light intensity of direct sunlight.
	Direct sunlight	In the path of direct rays of the sun.

happy or not under the light conditions provided. The drooping lack-lustre leaves which indicate that the plant is not getting enough light do not appear overnight. The table above describes natural light conditions suitable and unsuitable for palms indoors.

To convert a poorly lit room into a suitable abode for palms one must increase the available light. This may mean providing a fluorescent or incandescent light within a few feet of the plant. Setting up indoor plant lighting is a whole study in itself and you should consult experts in the field if you are interested in this solution. Sometimes there are more straightforward answers to the problem of lighting, such as pruning the foliage outside a window to allow more natural light to enter the room. Windows facing a fence or wall are usually poor light catchers. A coat of white paint on the fence or wall is a simple way of increasing the light reflected into the room. Painting the inside walls of the room white or a pastel shade has the same effect.

Water: How much water should one give a potted palm and how often? Palms need a lot of water when they are actively growing. If the conditions indoors encourage active growth, then watering should be frequent and generous.

Unfortunately such ideal conditions indoors are uncommon. It is therefore necessary to assess the environment when deciding how to water your palms. In the hot, dry air of well-heated rooms plants lose a lot of water through leaf transpiration. Under these conditions palms, like other plants, require frequent watering and benefit from a rise in humidity. In cool rooms growth is slow and water requirements reduced. Remember, a palm achieving little growth will survive with very little water.

In order to estimate a palm's water requirements you should consider also the type of potting mixture used. A potting mix made porous with sand or vermiculite will drain easily and tend to dry out rapidly unless other water holding components are present. It thus requires more frequent wetting than a soil or peatmoss-based mixture. If the potting medium holds water for weeks then it is perhaps too heavy. A dormant palm sitting in a waterlogged soil often succumbs to root rot.

A symptom of waterlogging or over-watering damage in most plants is wilt. Unfortunately, when confronted with this symptom, the owner too often gives the plant still more water, thus ensuring its demise. Overwatering palms causes the leaf tips to brown off. Wilt may be more difficult to observe in palms than in other plants because of their stiffer leaves.

Potted palms sometimes become "rootbound": the mass of roots has become so voluminous as to take up the whole space of the pot. Such a palm requires more water than the plant which still has room for further root development.

There are so many factors in the palm's environment to be considered that setting any rules for watering is almost impossible. One should reassess the palm's needs every three or four days and decide accordingly. To test the degree of moisture, insert a finger into the soil down to about three centimetres. If the soil feels moist then no water is needed. Water only when the soil feels dry. If other environmental conditions are already limiting the growth rate, then it may be advisable to apply only enough water to keep the soil barely evenly moist. Do not allow the soil to dry out completely as that would damage even a dormant palm.

Actively growing palms will benefit from an occasional drenching. Acids tend to build up in the soil around the roots. Drenching the soil once or twice a year will leach out these acids. When drenching the soil, allow water to run easily away from the bottom of the pot. You will need to apply the water for four to five minutes to allow salts to dissolve and be flushed away.

Four methods of increasing humidity:

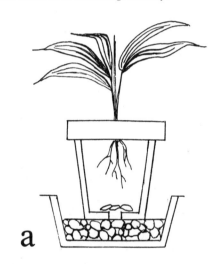

(a) Potted palm sitting on top of a tray of pebbles in which water has been poured.

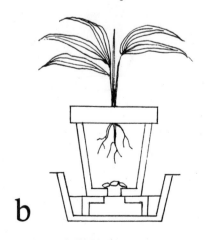

(b) Potted palm sitting on stand in tray of water.

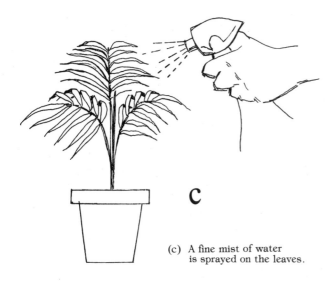

c

(c) A fine mist of water
is sprayed on the leaves.

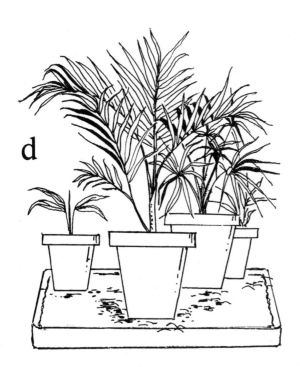

d

(d) Grouping plants increases the humidity
around the foliage.

Humidity: Moisture in the air is measured on a scale called "relative humidity". A relative humidity of zero per cent corresponds to absolutely dry air and 100 per cent to saturated air. As the temperature rises, more moisture is needed in the air to maintain any particular level of relative humidity. In other words, as the temperature rises the air becomes "drier" unless water is supplied.

The relative humidity indoors is usually low, particularly when the room is heated. Palms will survive for quite long periods in a relative humidity as low as 20 or 30 per cent. After several weeks or months of these conditions, however, they droop and lose their lustre and the tips become brown and ragged. A relative humidity level of 60 to 80 per cent is ideal for palms. This would be difficult to create throughout the room, but there are some easy methods of increasing humidity locally around the plant's leaves.

Hand spraying the leaves with a fine mist of water will humidify the plant for a short time. But most people do not have the opportunity or patience to mist their plants several times a day. An easier solution is to stand the pot in a shallow waterproof tray or dish in which a layer of pebbles at least four or five centimetres deep has been placed. Pour water into the dish without letting the water level rise above the top of the pebbles. Place your potted palm on the pebbles. The water in the tray will evaporate and maintain a certain humidity around the plant's foliage. It is important to maintain the water level just below the top of the pebbles. Water must not be seeping into the pot or the plant may become waterlogged.

A variation on this method is to use a tray filled with water and to sit the pot just above water level on a piece of wood or any stand of the same size.

Another way of increasing the degree of humidity is to group the plants. The mass of foliage seems to trap some of the water which the leaves produce by transpiring. This results in a more humid atmosphere around the plants than in the rest of the room.

Temperature: For every plant there are temperature extremes beyond which it cannot

Top: The sago palm, *Cycas revoluta* — in fact a palm imposter.
Above left: *Chamaedorea metallica* has metal-green simple leaves.
Above right: *Chamaedorea ernesti-augusti.*

Top: *Phoenix reclinata* clumps to form a fine shady stand.

Above left: *Licuala peltata* has leaves like great, green, circular discs.

Above right: *Pritchardia thurstonii* — a striking silhouette against the sky.

Top: In tropic and sub-tropic areas palms can be grown under the shade of other trees.
Above left: *Chamaedorea elegans* — well suited to tub or indoor culture.
Above right: *Chamaedorea microspadix* — its leaves have a velvety appearance.

Top: *Phoenix roebelenii* has a thick crown of fine leaves.
Above left: The traveller's palm, *Ravenala madagascariensis.*
Above right: Golden cane palms dress the set in the Sydney Opera House's
Bennelong Restaurant.

survive. One can also determine for each plant an optimum temperature range for active growth. The optimum range is highest for tropical plants. For the tropical palms it is from about 25°C to 35°C (77°F to 95°F). Modern homes in Australia and New Zealand generally maintain daytime room temperature between 18°C and 25°C (64°F and 77°F). Tropical palms will usually tolerate these temperatures quite well and maintain their condition although growth may be negligible. Nevertheless if night-time temperatures drop below about 13°C (55°F), some tropical palms may be damaged.

Indoor temperatures better suit palms originating from subtropical and temperate climates. A night temperature as low as 13°C (55°F) followed by day temperatures up to 25°C (77°F) provide a range conducive to some growth provided other conditions of light, water and humidity are satisfactory. The parlour palm (*Chamaedorea elegans*) and the Kentia palm (*Howea forsteriana*) are well suited to these indoor temperatures. Little growth will occur when the plants remain constantly for long periods in temperatures below 16°C (61°F). Cold draughts and sudden low frosty temperatures can damage leaves. Hardy palms such as the *Phoenix* palms, *Livistona* palms, windmill and European fan palms tolerate low temperatures very well. If room temperatures drop even to 5°C they will survive quite happily. For these hardy palms the level of light available indoors is more likely to be the growth-limiting factor.

Fertilisers: The potted palm growing indoors rarely grows fast. For this reason it must generally be fed in small amounts and infrequently. Only actively growing palms in summer temperatures can use nutrients quickly.

It is best not to fertilise a newly purchased palm until it has settled into its new environment. As this may take a month or more, you have the time to observe its growth rate. If fresh leaves are developing then you may experiment with additional feeding.

Fertilisers are nutritional boosters. Plants growing in nutritionally well-balanced soil mixes do not really require extra nutrients. Their growth may, however, be boosted by providing more nutrients. This "force feeding" is effective only when light, water and temperatures are held to optimal levels. In normal indoor conditions force feeding is overfeeding and can be a fatal mistake.

Two kinds of fertilisers must be distinguished: organic; such as manure, fish meal and other decomposed animal matter, decaying leaf matter, blood and bone; and chemical (or inorganic), which are concentrated mineral salts. Chemical fertilisers list their mineral constituents on their labels. If you are using a chemical fertiliser it is advisable to use a "complete" one which has the three main major elements, nitrogen, phosphorus and potassium as well as most of the minor elements, such as calcium, magnesium, sulphur, iron, manganese, boron, copper and zinc. Trace element (or minor element) fertilisers can be used as a supplement to those fertilisers already incorporated in the soil mix.

As explained in chapter 6, fertilisers can be incorporated into the potting mix. Repotting is the ideal occasion to add a longer acting fertiliser to the medium. I use a well-rotted cow manure as the main fertilising ingredient. Palms can be potted into 25 per cent cow manure without damage. Either organic or chemical fertilisers can be used in a potting mix.

Soluble fertilisers are easy to apply to potted plants. The nutrients completely dissolve in water and thus reach the whole root system. A growing palm may be fed with a soluble fertiliser every 3 or 4 weeks. Be careful to use only the strength recommended on the packaging. Do not be tempted to give an overdose.

Some soluble fertilisers may be absorbed to some extent directly through the leaves. Foliar feeding (spraying fertilisers on the leaves) is another method of providing nutrients to potted plants. A poorly nourished palm will respond quickly to this treatment and leaves will colour up green within a week or two. Foliar feeding can also be used on larger palms growing in the garden.

Insect pests

A healthy, well-nourished and well-grown plant is much less likely to suffer from an insect problem than a poorly grown plant. However, even a healthy leafy palm may still be troubled by a pest which is prevalent. In such a case, its condition slowly deteriorates unless control measures are taken.

Three main insect pests commonly affect potted palms.

White palm scale: This tiny sap-sucking insect has several other natural host plants. The scale insects feed from their usual position out of sight under the leaf. As they are easily missed, the foliage may start to show damage before you realise there is any problem. Early infestations can be detected by looking for the tell-tale irregular or circular yellowish areas which develop on the upper surfaces of the leaves. Several infestations may occur during the year and it is often possible to see a white cottony secretion, or even the individual white waxy scales formed by the insects for their own protection, on the underside of the leaf.

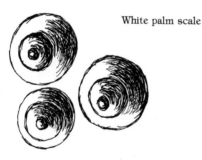

White palm scale

Mealy bug: These small sucking insects covered with a white fluffy wax also attack the undersides of leaves where they remain unnoticed until they have increased in

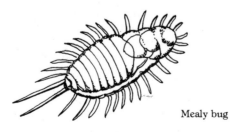

Mealy bug

numbers enormously and the plant begins to wilt. You will notice them singly or in small clusters of white cottony material. Mealy bugs are most common when the atmosphere is moderate to warm and moist. The high temperatures and humidity in glasshouses and ferneries are conducive to infestation. Mealy bugs secrete a sugary "honey dew" on which dark-coloured sooty moulds develop. Ants are attracted by the honey dew and feed upon it. The ants can transfer mealy bugs from one plant to another and spread the infestation. They may also assist in spreading the root-feeding mealy bug. By constructing galleries among the roots of the plants, they give access for the mealy bugs to fresh roots. The infestations usually build up most rapidly during late summer and autumn and decline in winter and early spring. Their life cycle may be completed as often as every six to seven weeks.

Red spider mite

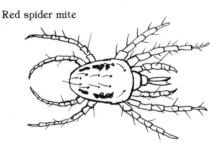

Red spider mite: This can also cause trouble to potted palms and other pot plants. It is an almost microscopic sap-sucking mite which feeds in great numbers on the undersides of leaves. The first sign of attack may be the appearance of yellow or brown speckles on the foliage. A fine webbing can sometimes be discovered on the underside of the leaf. A dry indoor atmosphere—especially in air-conditioned rooms—provides an environment very suitable for the red spider mite. The life cycle is complete in only ten days and breeding may continue all year round if the palm is kept in a protected position inside the house.

Control: White palm scale, mealy bug and red spider mite may all be controlled by dusting or spraying with the contact insecticide Malathion. This organophosphate insecticide is of fairly low toxicity and short residual life. It breaks down quickly after application and is no longer active after about one week. A white oil emulsion can be used as an alternative or as a supplement to Malathion. When using these chemicals, be careful to respect the instructions given on the packaging for use on ornamentals. If using Malathion and white oil together, make up the Malathion with water as directed and add about one tablespoon of white oil to each gallon of spray (or one teaspoon to every litre).

Particular attention should be given to the undersides of leaves when spraying the plant. Palms growing in pots may be placed on their sides. This will give easy access to the undersides of the leaves and will prevent the spray from dripping down the stem and accumulating at the base of the plant. In the case of red spider mite infestation repeat the treatment three days later and again ten days later.

It may be easier to sponge the leaves of individual plants lightly with a wet pad of cotton wool or a small sponge. Soapy water can be used but plain water is sufficient.

Ants should also be controlled especially to reduce root-feeding mealy bugs. An infestation of mealy bugs may be detected by withdrawing the plant from the pot to examine the roots. Scorching of leaf tips may also indicate the presence of mealy bugs, though this is not a definitive indicator as scorching may be caused by a variety of factors. Soil drenches may be used to control root-feeding mealy bugs. It is important to use enough liquid to wet the root zone properly. Malathion can be used as an effective soil drench at the same strength as that used for spraying foliage.

Fungal diseases

Compared to other cultivated plants palms are very resistant to fungi. But newly germinated palm seedlings sometimes develop a root-rotting fungal disease which severs the new root. Dusting seeds with a general fungicide usually helps reduce this problem. Leaf spot diseases, false smuts and leaf scab diseases are uncommon but damaging problems. In such cases, copper oxychloride powder such as Cuprox or Bordeaux diluted with water to recommended strength should be sprayed on to the leaves.

Nutrient deficiency

Deficiencies of certain minerals may be manifest in several ways. They usually cause a general yellowing of the palm but in some cases lead to a dwarfing of the whole plant or stunting of the newest leaves. Little research has been done on mineral deficiency diseases of palms and so specific symptoms are too uncertain to define. Fertilising with complete organic or inorganic fertilisers will guard against deficiencies. Nitrogen, phosphorus and potassium are required in much larger amounts than the other elements. If the soil is too acid or too alkaline then certain nutrients may be unavailable to the plant. Palms are in general tolerant to a fairly wide range of soil acidity and alkalinity.

Summary.
Important points on care and maintenance of the indoor potted palm:

1. Rotate your palms between indoors and a shady sheltered outdoor position.
2. Try to provide filtered or indirect bright light.
3. Water frequently only if the palm is growing actively, otherwise water only to keep the soil damp.
4. Rooms with a daily temperature variation between 13°C and 25°C are acceptable. Higher temperatures are more preferable.
5. Fertilise only in the active growing time.
6. Potted palms grown indoors are susceptible to pest attack. Check the undersides of leaves regularly for white palm scale, mealy bug and red spider mite. Spray or wipe the leaves to prevent or fight infestation. Treat chemicals with caution and always as directed on the packaging.

PALMS IN THE GARDEN
5

As a result of the recent revival of the interest in palms, more and more are now being planted as garden trees. Various palms are being used in the landscaping of new homes as well as in the renovating of old gardens. In Australia they are also popular as street trees. The use of palms in an outdoor setting should be planned carefully. It is too easy to get carried away with enthusiasm for the many and various types of palms. This enthusiasm often leads to haphazard planting resulting after a few years in a featureless jumble of foliage. Some important points must be considered when planting palms. The soil properties including drainage, the availability of water and shade as well as the final dimensions of the palm should determine the choice of the site.

The choice of palm

When buying a palm for the garden it is wise to find out what it will look like as it develops. The juvenile foliage, however attractive it may appear, gives no sure indication of the dimensions of the mature plant. The American cotton palm (*Washingtonia robusta*), for example, changes completely in appearance from youth to maturity. The young plant grows very slowly for five or more years producing new leaves which give the plant a rounded crown of bristling green fans. However, within ten to fifteen years it becomes a tall slim single-trunked tree with a ball-shaped head of leaves. *Washingtonia* palms are therefore not a good choice for small gardens but need a wider vista to be shown to advantage. The Canary Island date palm, on the other hand, develops from a relatively small pot plant to a spreading spiky massive plant perhaps four or five metres wide before developing a trunk. Therefore it needs a large area to develop, at least four metres from other plants. Canary Island dates have been used extensively as street

trees in Australia. Sometimes, because of lack of foresight, they have been planted under power lines. In such cases they invariably end up being pruned—an operation which too often disfigures them—or even removed.

Soil preparation and planting

Apart from sufficient space, palms also require good drainage. In many of their native habitats they live under high rainfall conditions but in soils which drain quickly. Only very few palms, such as *Sabal,* grow under swampy conditions. As for the type of soil, it is less important but does influence growth. Palms thrive in a rich soil which provides a large quantity of decomposing organic matter. They tolerate a wide variety of soils but prefer neutral to slightly acid soils. Highly acid soils should be treated with lime (calcium carbonate) to reduce the acidity to at least 5.5 or 6 on the pH scale. Similarly alkalinity prevents palms from obtaining from the soil all the minerals they require for growth and health. An alkaline soil can be made neutral to acid by dressings of iron sulphate or sulphur.

Be careful to prepare as large a hole as possible for each palm you plant and to layer the bottom with compost and other rotting material such as kitchen refuse or animal manure. Be careful too not to break the root-ball as you place the palm in the hole. Tread down the soil you place around the palm to avoid large air pockets. The palm should be planted slightly lower in the ground than its original position to encourage new root growth from the base of the trunk. This is particularly important 'when planting large mature palm trees. After planting the site must be thoroughly soaked and watered again after a few days, particularly if the soil dries quickly. In the case of large trees the soil must be kept well watered for at least one month to encourage new root growth.

Compared to other plants palms transplant well. Their fibrous root system gives them an advantage over other plants which send down a main (tap) root. Planting and transplanting should take place in summer months when growth is active and new roots have a chance to develop quickly. When removing a garden palm from one place to another, make with a spade a circular cut in the earth with a radius of 10 centimetres around the base of the palm to the depth of the spade. Water the plant well and leave it in its original site for another two weeks. This will allow new roots to develop from the base within the circle you have cut. When you remove the palm, take as much soil as possible with the root ball. The new roots should establish the palm in its new home without setback. Large mature trees will require deeper cuts than are possible with a hand spade. Huge palm trees have been successfully transplanted using heavy duty equipment such as cranes and semi-trailers.

The best planting site for immature palms supplies partial shade or dappled sunlight. A few young palms do better in direct sunlight but most prefer shade. Check the information on individual palm species before you plant. Palms such as *Linospadix monostachya,* the walking-stick palm, require deep shade to maintain lush green foliage. Most *Chamaedorea* species prefer shade to direct sunlight. In their natural state they shelter under the leaf canopy of the rainforest. The *Archontophoenix* palms prefer shaded conditions when they are young but reach for open sunlight as their trunk carries them skywards. In their natural state their leafy crowns form part of the rainforest canopy. Most *Phoenix* palms can adapt to bright direct sunlight from their youngest stages. They thrive in open sunny positions from the time they are first planted out.

Fertilising

Manure and compost in the soil surrounding a palm is the best form of fertiliser. Chemical fertiliser can also be used with success once the plant is well established and growing. It can be applied in liquid form or plugged into the ground surrounding the base of the palm. The latter method is most suitable for fertilising large palm trees. A "complete" chemical fertiliser or an organic fertiliser can be used. Another method consists of sprinkling fertiliser into an irrigation channel around the tree and watering it into the soil. Cultivating the topsoil around the tree for the first couple of years will keep the soil aerated and benefit the new roots. You can experiment with the amount of fertiliser you give your garden palms but always soak the ground well several times during the weeks following fertiliser application. To keep your palms in peak condition, apply 0.5 to 2 kilograms of fertiliser at a time for small to medium palms and 2 to 5 kilograms for large trees.

Frost-hardiness

Being tropical plants, the majority of palms do not tolerate severe or prolonged cold conditions very well. Nevertheless a good number of palms withstand freezing conditions without any more damage than some leaf burn. You should assess your garden's microclimate and experiment with plants reputed for their sensitivity to cold. Check the information available on each particular species before planting. Palms like *Butia, Chamaerops, Howea, Livistona, Rhapis, Trachycarpus* and *Washingtonia* resist freezing conditions and consequently adjust to a wide range of climates. *Arecastrum, Caryota, Chrysalidocarpus* and *Roystonea* palms tolerate cold conditions but may succumb to a heavy frost.

Pruning

Many palms have the tendency to hang on to their dead leaves. An annual trim keeps them looking their best. The *Phoenix* palm eventually drops its dead leaves but the tree does look better if the dead grey leaves are cut off and the old leaf bases are trimmed back to draw an interesting pattern on the trunk. The Canary Island date palm shows a characteristic diamond pattern when the leaf stubs are cut back to the same level each year. *Washingtonia* palms often hang on to their leaves for years, clothing their trunk with a characteristic "petticoat" of dead leaves. While some people prefer to leave the petticoat intact, others prefer a clean trunk. It is a matter of personal preference whether you trim back dead leaves or not. Some palms, *Archontophoenix* for example, do the pruning for you by dropping their dead leaves. The wind also often removes most of these.

Landscaping

When planning for the introduction of palms into a garden, one should always consider certain aspects of landscape design. Some palm trees, particularly the tall upright majestic *Roystonea, Sabal* and *Phoenix* palms demand to be segregated from plants whose foliage competes and clashes. They can on their own command a particular aspect of a garden landscape. Other palms look particularly well in avenues. *Washingtonia* palms look best placed far enough apart so the foliage of neighbouring trees doesn't interfere with their own. Cocos palms (*Arecastrum romanzoffianum*) are widely used as street trees in northern New South Wales and Queensland's Gold Coast. Planted closely together so that their foliage mingles, they make splendid avenues. On the other hand Canary Island date palms look good as avenue trees if positioned at least 12 metres apart so that their foliage does not overlap. Macquarie Street in Sydney shows on one side a beautiful line of Canary Island dates which give a touch of elegance to that part of the city.

Groups or clumps of palms can look beautiful in a large garden, on the edge of a lake, a seashore or a river stream. *Phoenix reclinata* has a natural clumping habit, each trunk leaning at a slightly different angle. Clumps of this palm give a tropical touch to a garden, particularly if planted by a pool.

Broad-leaved plants harmonise particularly well with the foliage of a clump of palms whose striking visual effect they tone down. Soft rounded foliages are most suitable to counterbalance the strong impact of palm foliage. When planting groups of the same palm—particularly if it is tall-growing—it is advisable to plant specimens of different sizes. From an aesthetic point of view, a harmonious tiering of trees is more graceful than a uniform line of specimens of the same height and proportions, as variety creates interest while uniformity generates boredom.

The windmill palm (*Trachycarpus fortunei*) and the European fan palm (*Chamaerops humilis*) are best planted as individual feature plants to be admired for themselves without distraction. A good way of enhancing them is to place them against a simple white wall or any other plain backdrop.

In a garden or a park, palms give more than the illusion of a cool retreat. In fact the temperature under a stand of palm trees is usually several degrees lower than in the shade given by other types of foliage. Clumps of Senegal date palms (*Phoenix reclinata*) will shelter a park bench efficiently. They are popular plantings in some of Australia's public parks. In Sydney's Hyde Park especially, a splendid stand of these palms gives shade to the city workers in search of some freshness during lunch hour.

GROWING PALMS FOR HOBBY OR PROFIT
6

The hobby gardener will usually, at some point, dream of growing plants for profit. There is however a deep chasm between the dream and the reality. Nurseries cannot be stocked by backyard production. The amount of time, effort and money required in preparing to open a plant nursery is enormous. To grow your own stock for retail as well as wholesale is an even bigger undertaking. Most plant shops deal only with the retail side of the business. Large nurseries usually employ considerable capital and staff, necessary for both enterprises.

Palm growing also requires considerable patience. To reach a saleable size, palms need more time than a lot of other plants. Two to three years are necessary to grow most palms from seed before they reach the right size. Some palms even need four or five years of growth to gain top prices.

Whether you are growing on a large scale in a commercial nursery or in twos and threes in your own shadehouse, the principles of culture are the same. However, the techniques of commercial growing are dictated by the need to save time. A nursery cannot afford to wait years for seeds to germinate or for seedlings to reach a saleable size. Notwithstanding the need for expediency in commercial growing, the following aspects of cultivation apply equally to hobby and profit growing.

Propagation from seed

Palm fruits usually contain only one seed. They vary in size, colour and by the amount of flesh enveloping the seed.

Fruits should be collected ripe, either directly off the plant or once they have fallen. A simple way of testing whether the fruit is ripe and the seed ready for planting is to use a sharp knife and cut cleanly through the fruit.

If the seed inside is soft and easily cut, it is not yet ready. If the seed is hard and its contents firm, then it is ripe enough to be planted.

Leaving the fruit too long on the tree or after collection can also be a mistake. The embryo will dry out and germination will be slowed. Soaking of dry seed in water usually overcomes the difficulty and triggers germination. Seed merchants may sometimes unavoidably provide dry seed which is several weeks or even months old. In such cases the seed contents may have begun to shrivel. If so, soaking is the first thing to do. Seeds difficult to germinate may require filing of the outer shell to allow moisture to enter.

Seeds sometimes carry various fungi which rot them or attack the germinating embryo. To reduce this risk, dust the seeds with a fungicide powder.

A shaded position in the garden provides a suitable spot for planting the seeds. When planting seeds, bury them to an even depth at least equal to their own length. If planted too shallowly they may dry out as the soil above them dries. The enthusiast and the commercial grower use seed boxes made from non-decomposable material. Ripe seeds give the best germination results. However, the medium used in the seed box influences the process. I have found 100 per cent river sand as successful as any other medium. But wet sand is heavy to move around. Some growers prefer a sand-soil medium. The addition of peatmoss to the mixture helps reduce the need for daily watering as peatmoss holds water well. A commonly used medium is sand, peatmoss and vermiculite in equal proportions. This combination provides a fairly sterile medium which protects the germinating seeds from fungus diseases.

Covering seed trays or boxes with a plastic sheet helps cut water evaporation to a minimum and aids the germination by raising the temperature inside the boxes. For good

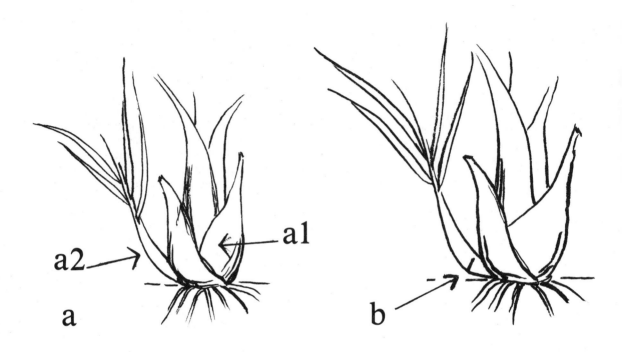

a

a2

a1

b

Removal of sucker
(a) 1 Parent stem
    2 Sucker

(b) Partially cut through sucker at this point.

germination some palms, particularly the tropical ones, need heat. Commercial growers often use a bench laid with heating cables to give "bottom heat" to the seeds. The soil temperature is controlled at approximately 24°C by a thermostat. Any temperature in the range 20°C to 28°C is usually satisfactory.

Palm seeds are generally slow to germinate. However, while most of them will take up to three months and a few species up to one year to germinate, some will germinate in under four weeks if ripe and placed in favourable conditions.

Vegetative propagation

Some palms produce offshoots or suckers from the base of the stem. Such palms are said to have a suckering or clustering habit. They are often called "multi-stemmed". Among others the golden cane palm (*Chrysalidocarpus lutescens*), lady palm (*Rhapis excelsa* and *R. humilis*) and some of the *Phoenix* palms show such a habit. The young suckers may be removed and planted separately for a new plant to develop. It is faster to obtain an advanced plant by this way than by growing it from seed.

Kentia palms and *Impatiens* share a shady corner.

The golden cane palm, *Chrysalidocarpus lutescens*

Top: An impressive row of *Washingtonia filifera*, the American cotton palm.
Above left: *Washingtonia* palms are often called petticoat palms — bearing
petticoats of dead leaves below the crown of the new.
Above right: *Pritchardia thurstonii*.

Left: A compatible grouping of *Spathiphyllum*, African violet and *Rhapis* palm.

Right: The golden cane palm when in sunshine develops a golden colour.

(c) New roots develop.

(d) Remove sucker and plant.
    Remove all leaves except newest
    before planting.

Nurseries do not usually grow their palms from suckers. In a commercial context this method is not very practical as it largely depends on the amount of plant material available. *Rhapis,* for example, can be commercially propagated in large numbers from seed. However, the hobby growers wishing to add two or three lady palms to their collections will obtain a far more satisfying result by planting a few suckers. The suckers should indeed develop into beautiful plants within a couple of years. The alternative—growing from seedlings—means years of patience.

The date palm (*Phoenix dactylifera*) forms suckers naturally. Commercial groves of date palms are planted using suckers cut from the bases of selected plants. The suckers are usually large, four or five years old and have produced roots. They are removed with a chisel usually in summer or spring, and most of the leaves are cut off to facilitate planting.

To divide suckers from parent plants, use a sharp knife or saw and remove as much root material and soil as possible. Suckers which have not developed roots of their own are more difficult to grow. A good approach is to cut halfway across the underground part of the sucker and leave it attached to the parent plant for several weeks. This should stimulate roots to develop above the cut, the sucker needing an extra path to obtain nutrients. Once these new roots have developed, the sucker can be wholly removed and planted.

"Tubing" or "potting up" seedlings

When the palm seedling shows one or two well-developed leaves it is ready for "tubing" or "potting up". However, the same size pot or tube will not suit all seedling plants. Indeed the vigour of the seedling root growth varies from one species to another. The root of the *Phoenix* palms, for example, generally grows vigorously right from germination. The rather large roots penetrate deeply and spread into new soil quickly. *Washingtonia* palms, on the other hand, develop fine seedling roots which are contained for several months in a small area. The first pot you choose for your palm should be able to contain the roots until the following spring. A small plastic tube four or five centimetres wide will suit a *Washingtonia* seedling whereas a tube five to seven centimetres wide suits better a *Phoenix* seedling.

Within twelve months the root material will probably have filled the original tube and the roots may even emerge from the holes in the bottom of the container. You should then move the seedlings into a ten to fifteen centimetre wide plastic or terracotta pot. Palms can be held in tubes for many more months than necessary but growth will then slow considerably.

Potting mixes

Of first importance in any growing medium is good drainage. A potting mix can consist of as many components as ten but more commonly of only three or four. Sand is the basis of most potting mixes. It is sand which ensures most of the good drainage qualities of a mix. The other components commonly used are fertile soil, peatmoss, vermiculite, sawdust, perlite, pulverised tree bark, leaf mould and animal manures.

Commercial growers often use soil-less mixes because they are light and can be easily reproduced once the formula is set down. Soil is a highly variable component and for that very reason is sometimes excluded from a potting mix. Fertile soil does however possess built-in nutrients and its micro-organisms break down organic matter continuously, releasing essential nutrients to the plant. Plants in soil-less mixtures, on the other hand, require frequent artificial feeding.

A predictable potting mix is usually preferred by commercial growers. One that is sometimes used for palms is sawdust and sand. Measured quantities of organic and inorganic fertilisers must be added to it at regular intervals. Another favourite in the nursery trade is sand, peatmoss and vermiculite, which also requires regular measured applications of fertilisers.

For the home gardener and hobby palm grower here is a tried-and-true potting mix providing the slightly acid medium which suits most palms:

1 part fertile soil (preferably sterilised)

1 part bush or river sand

1 part peatmoss or mushroom compost

1 part well-rotted cow manure.

Ready-made potting mixes are available and are usually quite good. If you are an indoor gardener you may prefer this simple solution particularly if you have to work within the confines of the living room or balcony.

"Potting on"

The process of repotting plants into a larger container is called "potting on". For best results do your potting on in late spring or early summer. This will give the palm a new burst of growth, fresh growing medium being provided for its active roots.

When the roots of a palm are growing out of the bottom of the pot, the plant should be potted on. The root system having filled the pot, the plant is looking for a further source of nutrients. Some plants, however, have searching roots which reach out through the holes of a pot long before the container is crammed full of roots. You can check if the plant is rootbound by examining the soil with a fork or by lifting the plant out of the pot. Plastic pots are somewhat flexible and therefore a rootbound plant should come out cleanly with the contents held intact by the root system.

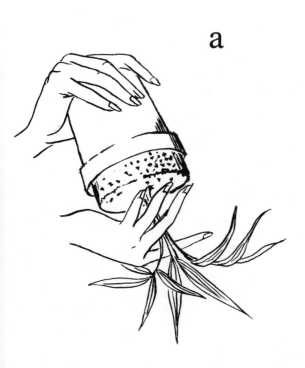

a

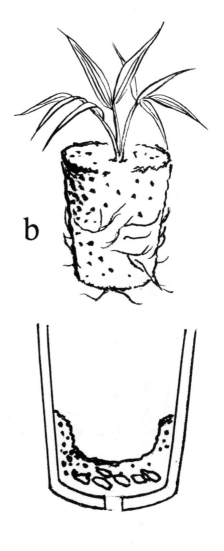

b

(a) Removing the plant from the pot.

(b) Choose a new pot with 2 or 3 centimetres extra growing space for the existing roots.

The new pot you choose should give two or three centimetres extra growing space to the existing roots. Resist the urge to use a large pot for a small palm. The root would take too long to utilise the soil and there is real danger of overwatering or overfertilising.

(c) Fill the outer space with fresh soil mix. Pack it down and water thoroughly to get rid of any air pockets.

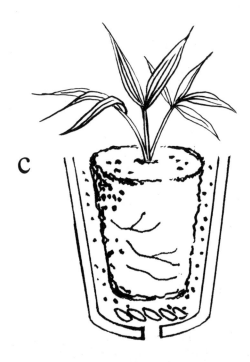

c

Feeding

Palms generally need a lot of fertiliser during the warm months, when they are growing. Feeding the indoor palm is explained in more detail in chapter 4.

Fertilisers suitable for palms include:
- "all-purpose" or "standard" fertilisers containing nitrogen, phosphorus, potassium and a variety of other elements
- blood and bone
- soluble organic fertilisers, for example Nitrosol
- soluble inorganic fertilisers, for example Aquasol
- well-rotted cow manure
- slow-release granular or "pill"-type fertilisers.

Often the components of a potting mix supply nutrients over a long period. Some useful examples are mushroom compost and well-rotted leaf mould.

Of course manufacturers' recommendations for dilution or mixing of any fertiliser must be respected. Irreparable damage can be done by application of overstrength fertilisers. If such a fertiliser has been sprayed, the leaves can show unsightly dead patches. If it has been applied to the soil, roots may die or be so damaged that growth is impaired.

Newly purchased or repotted plants do not require immediate feeding. If the potting mix does not contain soil, then fertiliser will be required within eight weeks. With a new purchase you cannot be sure that fertiliser has not been recently applied. Thus, if you are not prepared to repot the plant, you should wait before applying more nutrients. Here are general rules for feeding palms:

1. Apply fertilisers only in the warm months, when the palm is growing actively. In Australia and New Zealand this is approximately October to April.
2. To slow growers apply small amounts of fertiliser infrequently. To faster growers apply large amounts of fertiliser more frequently.
3. Water palms often in summer to keep nutrients in solution and drench occasionally to leach out accumulated salts.

Palms in the market-place

In Australia the big markets for palms are Sydney and Melbourne with the other capital cities of Brisbane, Adelaide, Hobart, Perth, Canberra and Darwin offering markets of substantial size. In New Zealand palms are popular everywhere, the North Island offering the best prospects for survival. Auckland and Sydney offer similar climatic conditions.

In Australia, Queensland offers the best growing climate for palms in its subtropical coastal regions. Large palm nurseries are concentrated in the region between the Queensland-New South Wales border and the Sunshine Coast, approximately 300 kilometres north. Nurseries further north are disadvantaged in being far away from the main markets, but this inconvenience is somewhat offset by conditions conducive to fast growth. In Sydney and Melbourne palm nurseries do operate but they have to use glasshouses to be able to compete with nurseries further north.

Large road shipments of palms from the northern nurseries are delivered into the southern markets. Brought from subtropical growing conditions where large quantities of fertiliser are used to ensure fast growth, these palms need acclimatising to the cooler southern conditions. Without a period of several weeks in the protected environment of the nursery's shadehouses the palms will suffer visibly, and may lose one or two leaves before accepting their new climate. The shock can be too great for some tropical palms and they may succumb. A half-way step between the subtropics and a temperate climate will preserve the decorative quality of the palm and allow it to adjust to a new environment.

Growing palms in the ground for later sale

This is a common practice in Queensland nurseries. Popular palms are planted out in rows for between four and eight years of growth. When they are large enough for sale, usually as landscape trees, they are removed from the ground. Some may even be seeding before removal.

The ground is usually prepared in such a way as to encourage roots to proliferate within a short radius from the base. A soil mix rich in organic material is used to fill the hole in which the palm has been planted. When the palm is removed several years later the roots are severed at about 20 centimetres from the base and the rootball is potted or wrapped in hessian. New roots will grow from the base of the stem into the soil retained.

Palms for hire

The plant-hire industry is fast growing and highly competitive. Invariably a small variety of palms appears on the plant listing. The service includes the replacement of plants which are visibly deteriorating, so it is then to be expected that the frequency of replacement is the main factor determining the hire cost to the client.

The dwarf date (*Phoenix roebelenii*), the parlour palm (*Chamaedorea elegans*) and the Kentia (*Howea forsteriana* and *H. belmoreana*) last well indoors. Their hire cost is therefore quite reasonable. The Cocos palm (*Arecastrum romanzoffianum*) does not adjust well to the indoor situation especially the uncaring environment of the business office. As a result, the Cocos palm is far more expensive to hire than most other palms. The Alexandra palm (*Archontophoenix alexandrae*) is popular, fast growing and usually relatively cheap to purchase. But indoor situations do not usually suit it, particularly where there is air-conditioning. For this reason the Alexandra does not often appear on the plant-hire list.

Plant-hire companies usually service their hired plants every one or two weeks. They check the soil for water requirements, clean down large leaves and generally tidy up the plant.

ARCHONTOPHOENIX

Two species, both native to Australia, are commonly available for purchase as pot plants: *Archontophoenix cunninghamiana,* the Bangalow palm, and *Archontophoenix alexandrae,* the Alexandra palm. The *Archontophoenix* palms have beautiful arching pinnate leaves and make attractive ornamental pot plants.

Both species are native to Australia's east coast, the Alexandra being found along the north Queensland coast while the Bangalow occurs further south along the coastlines of southern Queensland and of New South Wales to Batemans Bay. They are found in rather wet situations such as along river banks and in gullies.

Description

Both species are very similar in appearance. An easy way of distinguishing one from the other is by examining the leaf reverse. The underside of an Alexandra leaf is silver-grey while both sides of the Bangalow leaf are green. This feature is easily noticeable when the palm is young but is much more difficult to observe in a fully grown palm.

Archontophoenix trunks are quite smooth although ringed by the scars left by the fallen leaves. The mature palms may be 15 to 20 metres high and their leaves 1 to 2 metres long. Alexandra trunks are usually more swollen at the base than those of the Bangalow Palms. In both species fruit are small, round and bright red when ripe. The fruit bunches hang in beautiful showers of colour. The fruit stalk or spadix grows from the base of the crownshaft which is quite large and green in colour.

Suitability as an indoor plant

Archontophoenix palms only just qualify as suitable indoor plants because of their high light requirements. Therefore a window position is usually best. Be sure to place the palm in the position giving most indirect bright light. A patio or terrace able to protect the plant from wind and direct sunlight may be your best choice.

Suitability as a garden plant

As fast-growing palms *Archontophoenix* do best in rich moist soils. Give shade when young. The Alexandra is not very frost-hardy. The Bangalow shows more tolerance to cold and frost.

Propagation

Propagation is from seed. Germination occurs within three months from fresh ripe seed.

Special comments

The growth rate of the *Archontophoenix* is high in comparison with other palms. Large specimens are usually comparatively low in price but difficult to maintain indoors.

Archontophoenix alexandrae

ARECASTRUM ROMANZOFFIANUM

Previously known as *Cocos plumosa* or *Syagrus romanzoffianum* and commonly called Cocos palm, queen palm or plume palm. Originally from Brazil, it is a widely planted feather palm particularly popular as a garden plant on the east coast of Australia. The young plants make most attractive pot plants for indoor decoration.

Description

The young Cocos palm makes a very attractive indoor plant because of its unusual leaves. The early leaves are reed-like with definite parallel ribs but as the plant develops in its second and third year, the large simple leaves split apart and change into the characteristic "ostrich feather". These leaves, consisting of many fine leaflets, may range from stiff and ascending to curved and drooping. The mature palm can reach 8 to 10 metres, sometimes more, and the leaves are 2.5 to 5 metres long. The trunk, smooth but plainly ringed, is about 40 centimetres in diameter. The fruit, which hang heavily in clusters, are yellow to orange, fleshy and quite edible.

Suitability as an indoor plant

Cocos palms make a striking indoor pot plant particularly when 2 to 3 metres in height. They do however require bright indirect light which may be difficult to arrange indoors. A spell outside in a protected position providing dappled sunlight will refresh the plant and encourage new leaf development.

Suitability as a garden plant

These palms adapt to an open and exposed position but look better in partial shade. When mature they can resist temperatures as low as −8°C. Even young plants are frost resistant in certain limits. For fast growth Cocos palms require a lot of watering in summer.

Propagation

Ripe seed should germinate within three months. Heating may be necessary to encourage a good percentage of seed to germinate. Once potted the plants should develop rapidly if watering is adequate.

Special comments

Popular along northern New South Wales and southern Queensland coasts, Cocos palms make good avenues and groves. They transplant easily.

Top: *Livistona chinensis*, Chinese fan palm — a good landscape subject in a large garden.
Bottom: *Caryota* palms have a fishtail-type leaf, hence the common name of fishtail palms.

Top left: *Howea forsteriana*, the Kentia palm.
Top right: A *Cordyline*, the cabbage tree — a palm imposter.
Above: Chinese fan palms in an outdoor nursery.

Arecastrum romanzoffianum

BUTIA CAPITATA

Previously known as *Cocos yatay*. Commonly called wine palm and jelly palm because of the traditional uses of the palm fruit, *Butia capitata* is a drought-hardy palm native to Brazil and Uraguay. It makes a good plant for garden or veranda but does not flourish indoors.

Description

Leaves are pinnate in shape and a pale blue-green in colour. Leaflets are held rather stiffly in a pronounced V from the main leaf rib. The leaves of the mature palm arch strongly and are sharply pointed. The trunk grows to 6 metres high and can be half a metre in diameter. The old leaf bases remain attached around the trunk and can be quite long near the crown. Large heavy clusters of edible orange-coloured fruit hang from between the lower leaves.

Suitability as an indoor plant

A requirement for high light intensity makes the **Butia** unsuitable as an indoor plant, but it makes a good patio plant in a tub. Remember, however, that its spreading spiky leaves demand plenty of space.

Suitability as a garden plant

This palm is a popular garden and parkland tree. It makes an attractive single lawn specimen. It is very resistant to dry conditions and will withstand heat and drought quite well although it will not look its best under these conditions. It grows in almost any climate in Australia and New Zealand but does best where ample watering, rich soil and good drainage are provided. It resists frost and wind and is one of the few palms which maintain healthy leaves when growing along an exposed sea coast.

Propagation

Seed show some resistance to germination when the whole ripe fruit is planted. The most likely explanation is that the fruit contains an inhibitor to germination. I have overcome the problem by cleaning the flesh off the seed and bringing it to the boil in a saucepan of water before planting.

Special comments

Ripe fruits smell like pineapple and can be used to make wine or jelly.

Butia capitata

CARYOTA

Two species of the fishtail palms are commonly available: *Caryota mitis,* commonly called fishtail palm, and *Caryota urens,* known variously as fishtail palm, toddy palm and wine palm.
Popular indoor pot and tub plants. The unusual name "fishtail" refers to the shape of the leaflets.

Description

Both palms have beautiful long fern-like bipinnate leaves. The leaflets are themselves divided into smaller leaflets which present a characteristic triangular or wedge shape like a fish tail.

Caryota mitis is the smaller of the two fishtail palms. It is a multistemmed palm which produces new suckers when still a small pot plant. In the tropics one could expect growth up to 7 metres but much less in a temperate climate. *C. urens* is a larger single-stemmed palm. It grows to 15 or 20 metres in the tropics, much less in cooler climates.

Suitability as an indoor plant

Caryota palms can adjust to low light intensities which would be insufficient for most other palms. *Caryota mitis* has been widely used in large tubs for display in hotel foyers and reception halls.

Suitability as a garden plant

Though essentially tropical palms, *Caryota* grow in temperate regions where night temperatures are not consistently very low. Well-established plants withstand a few degrees of frost. Full summer sun can burn their leaves, so a shaded position should be preferred. A rich soil which drains well and plentiful water and fertiliser in summer months will provide the best growing conditions.

Propagation

Caryota mitis may be propagated by removing the suckers and growing them independently into new plants. Both *C. mitis* and *C. urens* are usually propagated commercially from seed.

Special comments

The *Caryota* species present an unusual flowering pattern. When the palm reaches maturity the first flowers appear from the top of the plant. Flowering and fruiting continues down the stem yearly from each leaf scar until the lowest fruits have ripened, and the tree then dies. With the multi-stemmed *Caryota mitis,* dying stems are being constantly replaced by new suckers and the plant is thus long-lived. The outer skin of the fruit is covered with stinging needle-like crystals which can be very painful to the touch.

In its native lands of India and Malaysia, *Caryota urens* is very useful. The pith of the trunk makes a good sago and great quantities of jaggery (a coarse brown sugar) are produced from the sap.

Caryota mitis

CHAMAEDOREA ELEGANS

Also known as *Neanthe bella* or *Collinia elegans.* Commonly known as the parlour palm. A dainty feather-leaved dwarf palm which has gained great popularity as an indoor plant. Particularly suitable for indoor positions where less than bright light is available.

Description

The parlour palm is a small, elegant indoor palm. Native to Mexico, its natural habitat is in deep rainforest under constant shade. If placed in direct sunlight the leaves quickly scorch. When grown in containers, the slender green stems seldom reach more than 1.5 metres. Each plant usually has six to eight finely divided pinnate leaves of a beautiful shimmering dark green. Flowers are orange and the small ripe fruit are black.

Suitability as an indoor plant

Parlour palms tolerate a range of light conditions indoors. They prefer warm humid conditions and therefore look best if they are sprayed with water as frequently as practicable. The soil should be kept moist but not wet for long periods. Keep the palm out of draughts as much as possible and do not ever place it in direct sunlight. When they are small, parlour palms look particularly attractive if grouped in a large container. At eighteen months the plants should be big enough to add to terrariums or dish gardens.

Suitability as a garden plant

In the garden the parlour palm may grow to 2 metres high. It is happiest in a sunless position but should do quite well if shaded from the midday sun. Beside a wall or fence facing south can be a good garden position, particularly if well protected from winds. Too much sun turns the leaves yellow. Continuous cold weather halts growth and frost damages leaves, but two or three degrees of frost should not kill the plant.

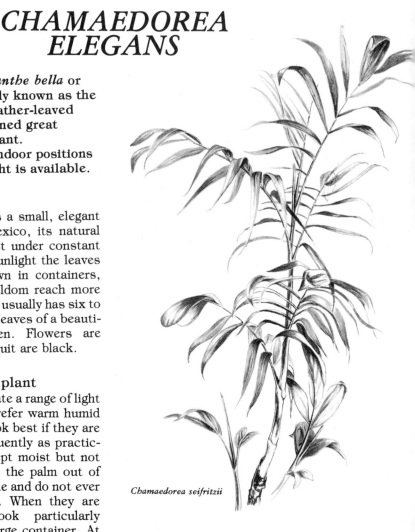

Chamaedorea seifritzii

Propagation

Male and female flowers develop on different plants. Successful seed production thus requires both plants. Ripe seed should germinate within two months.

Other *Chamaedorea* species

Chamaedorea erumpens and *C. seifritzii* are two popular suckering palms suitable for indoors. Both adapt well to fairly low light levels, such as a metre or two from a window. Refer to chapter 8 for more details.

Chamaedorea elegans

CHRYSALIDOCARPUS LUTESCENS

Previously known as *Areca lutescens.* Common names include golden cane palm, Areca palm and butterfly palm. An ornamental tropical palm from Malagasy, it forms a clump of stems and grows into a bushy-looking plant rather like bamboo. It makes a good pot plant but is best shown as a multistemmed plant in a large tub. Suitable for indoors or garden.

Description

The green and golden stems of this popular palm are ringed like bamboo canes. The leaves are pinnate, light green and 1 metre or more long. Elegantly arching and twisting, they cast beautiful shadow patterns. Growth to about 9 metres can be expected in the tropics but in temperate regions it does not exceed 2 to 4 metres.

Suitability as an indoor plant

A position providing bright reflected light is best. The golden cane likes humidity and your efforts to provide it will be rewarded in the beautiful foliage of this palm. A multi-stemmed golden cane in a large tub makes a splendid ornamental plant. Allow it to crowd the container and resist repotting unless the roots are forcing their way out of the container. Supply plenty of water in summer and do not allow the soil to dry out in winter. An evenly moist but not soggy soil will be best.

Suitability as a garden plant

Plant only in frost-free areas. The golden cane grows fast only in a tropical environment. A position giving partial shade or dappled sunlight is best. A shaded patio or terrace may be ideal for a tub plant.

Propagation

Male and female flowers are borne on different plants. Ripe seed should germinate within two months. You can also propagate by dividing a multistemmed plant. Remove the individual suckers with as much root material as possible before planting separately.

Other *Chrysalidocarpus* species

Chrysalidocarpus madagascariensis var. *lucobensis* is a tall tropical single-stemmed palm. Its leaves resemble those of *Arecastrum romanzoffianum.* It is suitable as an indoor pot plant or as a garden plant in frost-free areas.

The *Rhapis*, a lady palm — dainty finger-like leaves are a special attraction.

Top: *Archontophoenix*, Alexandra palms, in southern Queensland.
Bottom: The Australian palm, *Licuala ramsayi*.

Chrysalidocarpus lutescens

HOWEA

Two species, native to Lord Howe Island, are commonly available for purchase: *Howea forsteriana* (previously known as *Kentia forsteriana*) or thatch palm, and *Howea belmoreana* (previously known as *Kentia belmoreana*) or curly palm. Both are known in the nursery trade under the name of Kentia palms. There is no doubt that the Kentias are among the most suitable palms for indoor use.

Description

The leaves of very young plants show only a few separate leaflets. Plants four or five years old have much longer leaves each consisting of many dark green ribbed leaflets. The older leaves also demonstrate their graceful arching habit which is characteristic of mature plants. The growth rate of Kentia palms is rather slow; plants five years old may be less than 1 metre tall. For this reason Kentia palms are comparatively expensive.

Both *Howea* species grow to tall slender trees with smooth trunks scarred in rings by old leaf bases. *Howea forsteriana* is usually the taller, reaching 18 metres or more; *H. belmoreana* reaches about 9 metres. In their natural island habitat these palms grow tall because of the competition for light within the dense stands of palm trees, but away from their habitat, Kentia palms do not often reach their potential height. Around Sydney's suburbs they are only 3 to 5 metres high.

To distinguish the two species observe the leaf. *Howea forsteriana* has leaflets which turn downwards and droop softly, while *H. belmoreana* has upward-reaching leaflets held in an upright V shape.

Seeds are borne on long stalks hanging from among the lower leaves. Each seed is approximately 3 centimetres long, lemon shaped, hard and brown to red in colour when ripe.

Suitability as an indoor plant

Kentias are justifiably very popular in many countries as indoor potted palms. Young Kentia palms are very tolerant of low light intensities although they prefer bright indirect light. As potted specimens they continue to be used to decorate restaurants, hotel foyers and all kinds of public places, although often in these circumstances they live in less than ideal conditions of light and temperature. It is a practice among plant-hire companies to "spell" their valuable palms in shaded outdoor conditions to freshen the foliage and produce new growth. The home palm owner would do well to follow this practice.

Grouping several palms in the same pot tends to enhance the foliage. Keep the soil moist in summer and do not allow the soil to dry out in winter.

Suitability as a garden plant

Usually planted as individual garden trees, Kentias do look spectacular when planted in a group. Both *Howea* species tolerate low night temperatures and in fact do not grow well in a tropical climate. Both can sustain two or three degrees of frost.

Plant young palms in a shaded garden site to protect them from overexposure. Rich soil, good drainage and frequent watering give best results.

Propagation

Germination of seed can be slow and may take up to two years even when the seed bed is sufficiently heated. Sowing ripe seed coated with a fungicide powder helps to ensure that a high percentage of seed will germinate.

Special comments

A large seed industry is established on Lord Howe Island where Kentias are growing in abundance. In 1918 rats were brought to the island and remain to this day the biggest problem for the seed industry.

Howea forsteriana

LACCOSPADIX AUSTRALASICA

A promising newcomer to the nursery trade, this palm should make a good indoor pot plant. There is as yet no common name widely used. Being multistemmed, *Laccospadix australasica* makes an attractive display of dark green foliage.

Description

Naturally forming suckers early, *Laccospadix australasica* develops into a multistemmed clump within three or four years. The pinnate leaves are dark green and, even when the plant is small, are somewhat reminiscent of the Kentia. *L. australasica* does not gain height as quickly as the Kentia, probably because its energy is diverted into the growth of suckers.

Usually the main stem grows to approximately 4 metres before dying and being replaced by a younger stem in the clump. In their native habitat on the Atherton Tablelands of northern Queensland one will occasionally see a single-stemmed plant. The arching leaves develop to a final composition of 22 to 24 leaflets which droop downwards attractively.

The flower stalks are long pendulous spikes appearing from among the leaves. Small red fruit are a distinctive feature of the palm at its mature stage.

Suitability as an indoor plant

From a natural environment of tropical rainforest undergrowth, *Laccospadix australasica* shows tolerance to low light intensities. The commercial future for this palm looks bright as it appears to offer all the qualities of a successful indoor pot or tub plant.

Suitability as a garden plant

Laccospadix australasica has not yet been grown extensively as a garden plant. Found naturally between 600 and 1200 metres above sea level, it should be tolerant of low night temperatures in many regions of New Zealand and Australia. You can see several clumps of *L. australasica* growing in Sydney's Royal Botanic Gardens, although it is unlikely that these would have experienced frosts.

Propagation

Ripe seed remain viable for only a few weeks. Propagation may also be carried out by splitting off suckers and planting them individually.

Laccospadix australasica

LINOSPADIX MONOSTACHYA

Previously named *Bacularia monostachya,* the walking-stick palm is an Australian native plant, occurring furthest south of all Australian *Linospadix* species. A low-growing rainforest plant, it is tolerant of low light intensities and is thus suited to indoor light conditions. Its irregular ragged-ended pinnate leaves make it an unusual kind of potted palm.

Description

The distinctive feature of this small dainty palm is its slender trunk. Usually no more than 3 centimetres in diameter, it is that trunk which gave rise to the name "walking stick". In the rainforests of its native habitat you will find these palms reaching various heights up to 4 or 5 metres. The leaf stalks are short and the leaves are usually only 0.5 to 1 metre long. The unbranched arching flower spike can be very beautiful when in fruit. These fruit are small and of brilliant coral-red colour. Their flesh is quite edible.

Suitability as an indoor plant

It is possible to purchase well advanced walking-stick palms which have developed the fine trunk. However, for a pot plant I prefer the shorter-trunked specimens as their foliage gives them a more balanced appearance. Bright reflected light should be preferred but less will usually suffice. I have found the walking-stick palm very susceptible to red spider mite infestations. Frequent preventive spraying and water misting to maintain a high degree of humidity should keep the palm fresh and healthy.

Suitability as a garden plant

When choosing a position in your garden for this palm it is wise to remember that in the rainforest the walking-stick palm always lives well below the leafy canopy. It grows therefore in deep shade and in a rich mulching soil. In the garden total shade or filtered sunlight is suitable with protection from wind and frost if possible.

Propagation

Fresh ripe seed should be sown as soon as possible for best germination as seed does not remain viable more than two or three weeks.

Special comments

An Australian native of the east coast rainforests, *Linospadix monostachya* is found as far south as the Taree district of New South Wales.

Linospadix monostachya

LIVISTONA AUSTRALIS

Called cabbage tree palm or fountain palm, *Livistona australis* is popular all over the world. The large circular fan-shaped leaves make an interesting display. Suitable for a brightly lit large room, it makes also a good garden plant.

Description

Young plants two to five years old show spectacular soft green foliage. The leaves, deeply divided with leaflets tapering to a point and slightly drooping, look like open fans. Leaf stalks have short sharp spines but these are no problem in handling the plant. The palm remains small without forming a trunk for about six years and its leaves enlarge to perhaps 30 to 50 centimetres width. When fully grown the mature palm can reach 20 metres or more, and it has then a stout cylindrical trunk. The crown of leaves is round with large fan leaves drooping at the tips. The flower stalks are hidden among the leaves and the fruits, which are spherical, take a brown-black colour when ripe.

Suitability as an indoor plant

Cabbage tree palms can be grown in containers for many years. A large tub makes a suitable home for the palm until it has developed a short trunk. A position close to a window should give the plant enough light but a veranda or patio providing filtered or dappled sunlight is more suitable.

Suitability as a garden plant

Cabbage tree palms adjust to a wide range of climates. They are hardy to both frosts and severe heat. Leaves look greener and glossier if grown in semi-shade. Try to shelter young plants from frost and direct sunlight for the first three or four years. Heavy moist rich soils are best for garden plantings but cabbage tree palms will grow in a wide range of soils.

Propagation

Germination from ripe seed should take about one month. Seedling palms need plenty of organic fertiliser during the warm months of the year.

Special comments

Livistona australis grows naturally from southern Queensland to far eastern Victoria. It occurs further south than any other Australian palm species. Some fine stands of this palm can be seen around Sydney, particularly on the coast.

Other *Livistona* species

Approximately 16 native species of *Livistona* can be found in Australia. This genus of palms has by far the largest number of species in Australia, among which many remain unnamed while more are still to be discovered. Some species difficult to obtain are *Livistona drudeii* (north of Townsville, Queensland), *L. muelleri* (common at Cape York), and *L. laurifilla* (coastal Western Australia along the Kimberley Mountains). *L. decipiens* and *L. mariae* (described in chapter 8) may be a little easier for collectors to procure but are certainly not widely available.

Caryota palms are unusual in that they flower from successive nodes down the stem, after which the stem dies.

Above left: *Pinanga kuhlii* is a tropical beauty.
Above right: *Cyrtostachys renda* has attractive red leaf stems and leaf bases.
Above: Would it look so well without the palms?

Livistona australis

LIVISTONA CHINENSIS

Native to central China, this palm is known as the Chinese fan palm or Chinese fountain palm. With its beautiful spreading fan-shaped leaves it makes an attractive pot or tub plant and is probably the most popular indoor fan palm. It requires a fairly wide location for its spreading leaves and makes a beautiful single tree in a garden lawn.

Description

At the juvenile stage the palm looks strikingly attractive with its bright green shiny round leaves cut into many leaflets or segments. In the first two years these segments are few but leaves developing after three or four years show many more leaflets and a much larger span. The leaflet tips are pendulous and in the older plant look like hanging icicles. Leaf stalks are spined as with all *Livistona* palms.

The Chinese fan palm grows very slowly to an eventual height of about 10 metres but most often does not reach that height. The grey trunk is about 25 centimetres thick with leaf bases adhering near the top. The palm is most easily identified when mature by the fringe of drooping leaf tips surrounding the leaves.

Suitability as an indoor plant

This palm lives happily inside if given bright indirect light. The leaves increase in size with age and the plant may need a fair amount of space to be shown to best advantage. To encourage fresh growth, place the palm outside for a few weeks in shade or filtered sunlight.

Suitability as a garden plant

Being slow to grow—it may take ten years to form a trunk—the Chinese fan palm can be used as a shrub-like cover under other trees. Preferring shade when young, it will look its best if protected from direct sunlight. This palm is frost-hardy to approximately −7°C. Like other *Livistona* species it prefers a deep rich moist soil provided that it is well drained.

Propagation

Seeds should germinate easily within six weeks if planted when ripe.

Livistona chinensis

PHOENIX:
the date palms

There are many species of *Phoenix* palms. Only the most popular ones grown in Australia and New Zealand will be presented here.

It is well to remember when trying to identify any *Phoenix* palm that it may not be true to type. *Phoenix* species hybridise easily. The male and female flowers are borne on different plants. If different species are grown in close proximity then the seed resulting from cross-pollination will give rise to plants different from either parent. It is often best to describe a plant as, for example, *Phoenix reclinata* type or *P. canariensis* type. An excellent current guide to the botanical features of the *Phoenix* species is *Palms of the World* by J. C. McCurrach, published by Harper & Brothers, New York.

PHOENIX CANARIENSIS

The Canary Island date palm is a large robust palm suitable for growing in a tub or large pot for up to six years. It grows into a large tree of considerable grandeur. Popular around the world in gardens and avenues.

Description

The date palm can grow to a height of 20 metres but more commonly does not exceed 7 to 10 metres.

For the first ten years of growth this palm consists of a dense collection of long tough arching pinnate leaves radiating from ground level. The leaves, of a deep green colour, have many stiff leaflets, those at the base having the form of spines. The leaf crown may be as large as 7 metres across, so it is best to allow a lot of space, particularly when planting in rows. A well-grown mature tree may have between fifty and a hundred leaves. Bright orange fruits are carried in heavy bunches between the leaves. These fruits are edible though not tasty.

Suitability as an indoor plant

The harshness of the leaves does not help to make this palm popular indoors. However, as a display plant for a large room, entrance hall or foyer, it is an excellent choice provided that the palm is placed out of people's way. Indoors, the low light level will over a period of months give the plant a softer appearance as the leaves lose some of their rigidity. In the long term this palm does better outside or at least on a veranda or courtyard where it receives more light.

Suitability as a garden plant

The Canary Island date is more commonly grown in temperate and subtropical regions than in the tropics. Having a strong rooting system, it can be grown in just about any soil type. It responds well to heavy fertilising and watering in spring and summer. It will also survive a poor soil and period of dry conditions. In the garden it thrives on heavy mulching with manure and regular applications of commercial fertilisers. Young seedling palms can be planted in positions where they receive full sun or semi-shade. Tolerant of sea breezes and salt air, the Canary Island date palm has become a popular seaside tree. It resists both high and low temperatures as well as frost.

Propagation

Fresh seed germinate readily but growth is slow.

Special comments

Old leaves should be removed with a saw to keep the tree looking tidy. Dead leaves would otherwise remain attached to the trunk for years before eventually falling off. Regular cutting back of these dead leaves at their base results in a characteristic diamond pattern on the trunk.

Cycas
Circinalis

✓ § Sabal
Bernardana

✓ § Hyophorbe
Verschaffeltii

§ Corypha
Umbraculifera

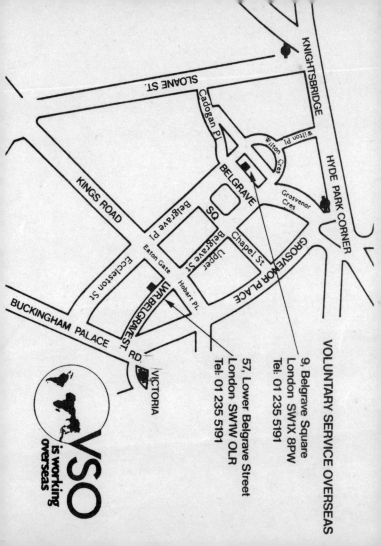

VOLUNTARY SERVICE OVERSEAS

9, Belgrave Square
London SW1X 8PW
Tel: 01 235 5191

57, Lower Belgrave Street
London SW1W OLR
Tel: 01 235 5191

VSO
is working overseas

KNIGHTSBRIDGE

SLOANE ST.

Cadogan Pl

Wilton Pl

Wilton Cres

BELGRAVE

HYDE PARK CORNER

Grosvenor Cres

KINGS ROAD

Belgrave Pl

SQ

Upper Belgrave St

Chapel St

GROSVENOR PLACE

Eccleston St

Eaton Gate

Hobart Pl.

LWR BELGRAVE ST.

BUCKINGHAM PALACE RD.

VICTORIA

Phoenix canariensis

PHOENIX ROEBELENII

A native of Vietnam, *Phoenix roebelenii* is commonly called the dwarf date palm, pygmy date palm or miniature date palm. Delicate and graceful, this small palm adapts well to low light levels and consequently to indoor conditions. It also makes a beautiful garden plant.

Description

Leaves are feather-like, about 1.5 metres long, curving and softly drooping at the ends. Each leaf has many fine leaflets and a few weak spines at the base. On a well-grown mature plant there may be as many as fifty leaves thickly clustered at the crown. Eventually reaching 2 metres or more, the trunk, which is composed of old leaf stubs, remains quite slender (approximately 12 to 18 centimetres in diameter). Sometimes suckers develop from the base of the trunk giving rise to new stems.

Suitability as an indoor plant

The dwarf date makes an excellent indoor pot or tub plant. Since the trunk takes ten years to develop, this palm has potentially a long life as an indoor plant. It is capable of adapting over a period of months to relatively low levels of light indoors. Little growth will however be achieved under these conditions. Only a position brightly lit with indirect or reflected light will allow the palm to develop. Keep the palm out of draughts as this can often dry out the leaf tips. Repotting should be necessary only every two or three years as the growth rate is usually quite slow indoors. Fertilise in summer only and water to keep the soil moist.

Suitability as a garden plant

The dwarf date makes a delightful shrub-sized garden plant. Its foliage will remain soft and graceful in partial or full shade. In full sunlight the leaves will become harsh and stiff but the palm will grow equally well. Established plants tolerate some very high temperatures as well as some frost.

Propagation

Propagation is by seed germination. Ripe fruit are small, black and olive-shaped. The seeds they contain readily germinate within one or two months.

Other *Phoenix* species

Phoenix dactylifera is by far the best known of the **Phoenix** palms. It is the commercial date palm. *P. reclinata* and *P. sylvestris* are species less well known to Australians and New Zealanders but equally successful as garden trees. *P. rupicola* is a sought after date palm with an established reputation as an indoor pot plant and now gaining popularity as a landscape palm. Refer to chapter 8 for more details on these palms.

Phoenix roebelenii

PTYCHOSPERMA

Two popular species are *Ptychosperma macarthuri,* called the Macarthur palm, and *Ptychosperma elegans,* known as the solitaire palm. Although both are more suited to tropical and subtropical climates they can make successful house plants provided they are given bright indirect light and are not subjected to long cold spells.

PTYCHOSPERMA MACARTHURI

Description

The Macarthur palm is a tropical multistemmed palm from New Guinea. The green ringed stems resemble bamboo canes. Older stems turn grey in colour. Leaves are pinnate, each with twenty or more pairs of bright green leaflets or segments.

The leaflets are broad and blunt with a "bitten off" appearance at the tips. Borne in grape-like bunches, fruits eventually turn from green to bright red.

Suitability as an indoor plant

The Macarthur palm's habit of constantly forming new stems makes it a good tub plant. It can be placed indoors if bright indirect light is provided and temperatures are kept around 18°C with increased humidity.

Suitability as a garden plant

Once the palm is several years old it takes full sun. Normally fast growing in the tropics, it grows at a rather slower pace in cooler climates. In a tropical garden the Macarthur palm will make a fine clump resembling a bamboo grove and will reach a height of about 3 metres. Occasionally in good growing conditions it can double or

treble that height. The Macarthur palm must be grown in frost-free areas and protected from cold winds.

Propagation

Successful propagation may be from seed or from division of the plant into individual suckers which will produce new plants.

PTYCHOSPERMA ELEGANS

Description

The solitaire palm has only six to eight leaves at any one time. The wide leaflets, held stiffly upwards, show jagged "cut off" ends. With its leaves arching strongly, the mature tree somewhat resembles the Bangalow palm. The solitaire palm rapidly develops a single trunk showing raised ring scars. Native to northern Queensland, it reaches 7 to 8 metres in its natural tropical environment.

Suitability as an indoor plant

Juvenile palms make good indoor plants with bright indirect light an absolute requirement. As with the Macarthur palm, indoor temperature conditions must be kept high, at 18°C or more. For healthy plants some humidity should also be provided.

Suitability as a garden plant

One solitaire palm makes a good palm for a small garden provided it does not have to suffer from frost and is protected from strong winds. Difficult to grow away from the tropics, it is nevertheless worth while.

Propagation

Propagation is from seed. Seed beds may be heated to ensure good germination.

Ptychosperma elegans

RHAPIS

Two species of lady palms are cultivated in Australia and New Zealand: *Rhapis humilis,* the slender lady palm, and *Rhapis excelsa,* the broad-leaved lady palm. Both are small multistemmed fan-leaved palms suitable for growing indoors, and also make good garden plants.

Description

The most attractive feature of the lady palm is the leaf. A glossy dark green colour, it is deeply divided and fan-shaped, with each leaflet a finger-like segment of the fan. The leaves of *Rhapis humilis* are divided into ten to twenty slender drooping leaflets. *R. excelsa* has leaves of five to eight leaflets which are more stiffly held and, as their common name suggests, broader than those of *R. humilis.*

Being quite thin, the stems of the lady palms look like bamboo canes. They are covered with hairy leaf bases and only the older stems are clean. Stems remain short for years but given good growing conditions can reach as much as 5 metres. However, half that height is more common. *Rhapis humilis* may only reach 1.5 metres. The clump of *R. humilis* is so dense that it is often difficult to see through the mass of foliage. This is not so for a clump of *R. excelsa* which is not nearly as bushy near the base.

Suitability as an indoor plant

Native to southern China, the lady palms were introduced to England in the late eighteenth century and have been popular indoor plants ever since. They are particularly suitable for indoor situations and adapt well to comparatively low light levels. Placed outside on a permanently shaded patio or porch they grow faster than when kept inside.

The growth rate of the lady palms is, in any situation, slow. Overfertilising is there-fore a risk. If the palm is growing in a rich soil mix then it should not be necessary to fertilise more than twice each year during summer. Saturate the soil when watering, but do not water if the soil is still wet from the last watering. Withhold water in winter until the top few centimetres of soil are fairly dry. Then water until the soil is moist.

Repot every three or four years while the palm is still growing. Once the palm has developed into a multistemmed plant, it may be kept in a tub for decades with only yearly top dressings to freshen the growing medium.

Suitability as a garden plant

Rhapis palms will grow in full sun but this tends to turn the leaves rather yellow. A partially shaded position should be preferred to keep the foliage green and glossy. *Rhapis* palms are very frost-hardy and will grow in a wide variety of climates. A single plant eventually develops into a dense multistemmed clump perhaps 2 metres across.

Propagation

As male and female flowers develop on different plants, fertile seeds are a little difficult and rather expensive to obtain. *Rhapis* are grown commercially from seed but even under optimal conditions seedlings grow only about half a metre in two or three years. A far more satisfactory way to grow new *Rhapis* palms is to plant the suckers. Growth is more rapid and a reasonably sized pot plant is obtained comparatively quickly.

Special comments

Rhapis palms are in under-supply and highly prized among palm collectors. Advanced specimens of ten or more years old are particularly expensive.

Rhapis sp.

TRACHYCARPUS FORTUNEI

Previously known as *Chamaerops excelsa,* the windmill palm is an attractive fan-leaved palm. It is extremely hardy in cold conditions and makes a good indoor, terrace or garden palm in temperate climates.

Description

The windmill palm has a regular head of fan-shaped leaves rather reminiscent of the windmill from which it takes its common name. Up to 1 metre in diameter, the leaves are deeply divided into numerous rather stiff dark green leaflets. Leaf stems are toothed but not spined as in the similar-looking European fan palm (*Chamaerops humilis*).

The single trunk, about 30 centimetres wide, is covered with a mat of thick brown fibres which look like horse hair. These fibres are produced as the leaf bases disintegrate. Once the trunk develops in a young plant the growth rate may be 15 to 30 centimetres yearly.

The large flowers are yellow. The small fruits which appear in masses amongst the foliage are blue-purple and grape-like.

Suitability as an indoor plant

Slow growing and decorative, wind-mill palms make quite good indoor plants. Bright light is a must for their indoor location and a frequent refreshment period outside will help bring on new growth. One month in a semi-shaded position in the garden during autumn or spring should suffice. As the trunk increases in height this palm becomes an excellent tub plant for terrace or courtyard.

Suitability as a garden plant

In the open garden the windmill palm lives through the most taxing of cold conditions including frost and snow. Grown outside at Kew Gardens, London, and in Edinburgh it fully deserves its claim of the hardiest of palms. The windmill palm attains best growth under a temperate climate. In hot dry climates the leaves can look quite ragged.

Windmill palms are often used as landscape subjects. Their trunk and head of leaves give them an interesting shape which can be well featured against brick walls.

Propagation

Seeds germinate well, usually within two months. Seedling growth is very slow.

Trachycarpus fortunei

WASHINGTONIA

There are two species of American cotton palms: *Washingtonia robusta,* also called Mexican fan palm, and *Washingtonia filifera* or Californian fan palm. Both are commonly planted large trees in Australia. They grow fast, requiring more light than is available in most indoor situations. They show handsome fan leaves with cotton-like threads hanging from between the leaf segments.

Description

Within two years seedling palms are showing their large fan leaves and red stems. Within four or five years the leaves which are then deeply divided into many segments become very large. As the tree matures the leaf segments start drooping. Fine cotton-like threads hang from between the leaflets giving the palm its name of cotton palm.

The trunks of the two *Washingtonia* species look quite different. While *Washingtonia filifera* has a wide massive trunk which grows to about 15 metres tall, the trunk of *W. robusta* is slender and reaches 25 to 30 metres in height.

A characteristic feature of the American cotton palms is their shag of dead leaves. This shag may be so persistent as to obscure the whole trunk. Sometimes it is blown down or cut down and only a few dead leaves may be visible. Trees growing in a garden protected from winds often retain their shag. The shag is sometimes called a petticoat, the trees being called "petticoat palms".

Suitability as an indoor plant

American cotton palms need a lot of bright light. This together with a fast growth rate makes them unsuitable for indoors. But they make excellent pot or tub plants to be placed in a courtyard or by a path or swimming pool.

Suitability as a garden plant

Both species are frost-hardy and can be grown under a wide range of climates from the tropics to desert plains. Liberal quantities of water and top dressing with manure will push along their growth.

Propagation

The small black seeds germinate readily. Seedling growth rate is fast, with fan leaves appearing within twelve months.

Washingtonia robusta

COLLECTORS' PALMS
8

Many of the beautiful palms prized by collectors come from tropical climates and require the special conditions of a warm greenhouse for successful cultivation. Here follows a list of some of these interesting palms which covers their main features and requirements.

Aiphanes caryotifolia: From South America. Grows into a slender tree of about 10 metres. Leaves have wide ruffled-looking leaflets and jagged ends. Trunk and leaves are covered in sharp black spines. Tropical growing conditions.

Areca catechu: The betel palm of South-East Asia. Slender trunk to 10 metres or more. Attractive pinnate leaves. The nut is chewed with lime as a mild stimulant. Tropical growing conditions required.

Arenga engleri: A dwarf palm with multiple trunks. Good for tub or pot in sun or shade. Hardy to frosts. Leaves are pinnate with leaflets in various shapes. Irregular edges. Stems covered with black fibre. The sap can be a strong skin irritant. Temperate and subtropical climates necessary for growth.

Calamus muelleri: Lawyer vine. One of several species of *Calamus* palms native to Australia. A climbing palm with spiny fine stems extending into the trees and attaching to foliage (or human clothing) using fine barbed appendages. Found in rainforests as far south as the mid-New South Wales coast. Suitable when a seedling as a decorative indoor pot plant.

Carpentaria acuminata: Native to the high rainfall areas of Australia's Northern Territory and a favourite palm in Darwin. The seedling palm is attractive with the first few leaves having just two lobes. Leaves formed later are pinnate like those of the Alexandra palm. The terminal leaflets are wider than the others and have four points. Suitable as an indoor plant under good light. Outside, a frost-free position is required, preferably in the tropics.

Chamaedorea erumpens: A bamboo-like palm which usually grows 2 to 3 metres, multiplying rapidly from suckers. It is a good indoor tub plant liking bright indirect light. Outdoors it scorches easily in full sun and is best grown in deep shade in tropical conditions but will adapt to cooler climates.

Chamaedorea metallica: A small palm with a slender trunk and large, leathery, metallic blue-green leaves. Makes an interesting garden plant.

Chamaedorea microspadix: A bamboo-like clumping palm with fine feathery leaves. Most attractive as a tub plant.

Chamaedorea seifritzii: Similar to *C. microspadix*. Makes a good pot or tub plant indoors. Young plants sucker easily and produce attractive pinnate leaves, the end leaflets larger than the others.

Chamaerops humilis: The Mediterranean or European fan palm. A slow-growing palm with stiff fan leaves. It will remain a small pot or tub plant for years. In the garden it suckers to form several trunks covered with a black hair-like material. Very hardy in cool climates and endures poor soil, drought, wind, heat and neglect.

Cocos nucifera: The coconut palm. Widespread in all tropical regions, it is the most populous of all palm species. Solitary leaning or curving trunk and long pinnate leaves. A coconut palm usually takes seven years to produce a crop and ten years before a significant number of coconuts are produced. Easily grown and transplanted in tropical climates, it does not however produce fruit or grow easily further south than Brisbane in Queensland. Popular as a landscape palm in Australia's tropical north.

The main commercial product is copra which is the dried "meat" of the fruit. Copra is used in the production of various oils. Sap can be drawn from the flower stalks for "toddy" which is used to produce sugar and alcohol. The outer husk of the fruit,

Chamaerops humilis

called "coir", is used to make twine, mats, brushes and coarse textile products. In former days the Polynesians made use of every part of the coconut for one purpose or another. Today it is an important food and its production and export make a large industry in the South Pacific.

Cyrtostachys lakka: The sealing-wax palm. A very beautifully clumping palm which forms several slender bamboo-like canes up to 7 metres high. The stunning feature of this beauty is the scarlet leaf stalks and leaf sheath. Native to the Malay Peninsula. This is an exotic well worth the effort of growing but requires a simulated subtropical to tropical environment.

Cyrtostachys renda: Similar to *C. lakka* but taller. Also has bright red colouring to its leaf stalks and leaf sheath.

Dictyosperma album: Commonly called princess palm. Originates from Mauritius. Has a solitary trunk and pinnate leaves which twist so that the leaflet tips are parallel to the trunk, a feature shared by the *Archontophoenix* palms. A variety of *D. album* called *rubrum* shows reddish veins in the new leaves of the young trees. Grows fast. The juvenile palm makes a good indoor plant.

Elaeis guineensis: Oil palm from tropical West Africa. Its seed oil is used for soap making and for fuel. The pinnate leaves and single rough trunk give a characteristic umbrella shape to the tree.

Hedyscepe canterburyana: Single-stemmed feather-leaved palm very similar to *Howea belmoreana.* Native to Lord Howe Island where it grows on the mountain sides. Difficult to obtain but will make a good pot plant.

Hydriastele wendlandiana: A tropical feather palm from the north coast of Queensland and the Northern Territory. A tall slender-stemmed palm growing best in partial shade and well-watered locations. Not suitable as a garden plant south of the Tropic of Capricorn.

Hyophorbe verschaffeltii: The spindle palm, previously known as *Mascarena verschaffeltii.* a bottle-shaped trunk and stiffly arched pinnate leaves make this palm singularly attractive in a garden setting. Also makes a good pot plant. Very tolerant of drought and salty soil.

Licuala grandis: Native to the island of New Britain in the South Pacific. This is a truly elegant palm suitable for a deeply shaded and wind-protected site in a tropical garden. A hothouse plant in other areas. The leaves are almost completely circular and undivided though strongly pleated. Produces a short trunk but grows very slowly.

Licuala ramsayi: Formerly *L. muelleri.* Found in dense stands in swampy coastal lowlands of the Queensland coast north of Cairns. It displays large fan-shaped leaves which are almost completely circular and are divided into only a few wide segments. It grows to 12 metres or more in its natural habitat but stays a small palm for many years in a deeply shaded position in a garden. Grows well in a wide range of climates.

Livistona: Approximately sixteen native species of *Livistona* are to be found in Australia. Many remain unnamed and doubtless there are still more peculiar to Australia yet to be discovered. *L. australis,* described in chapter 7, is the most common and best known species because of its eastern distribution along the New South Wales and southern Queensland coasts. A few of the other species native to Australia are *L. drudeii* (north of Townsville, Queensland), *L. muelleri* (common at Cape York), *L. benthameii* (tip of Cape York and Arnhem Land), *L. laurifilla* (coastal Western Australia along the Kimberley Mountains). *L. decipiens* and *L. mariae* may be a little easier to procure for collectors but are still not readily available.

Livistona decipiens: Grows naturally over a large area of the Queensland coast from Townsville to Fraser Island. Fan-shaped leaves have very fine drooping leaflets. Single-

Microcoelum weddelliana

stemmed and fast growing, it is suitable as a tub plant in a protected outdoor site.

Livistona mariae: An adaptable small fan palm found naturally in Palm Valley in the Macdonnell Ranges of central Australia. It prefers plenty of water but withstands dry spells. Called the red-tinged palm as the young leaves are a blood-red colour. Grows slowly but is frost-hardy.

Livistona rotundifolia: A cold-tender species which grows best in the tropics. Young plants are especially attractive because of their almost perfectly round fan leaves that droop softly at the edges.

Microcoelum weddelliana: Previously known as *Cocos weddelliana* and *Syagrus weddelliana.* This is a graceful feather-leaved palm native to Brazil. Usually does not reach more than 2 metres in height. Suitable as an indoor plant, it can be grown to maturity in a large tub and is ideal for a shaded patio or veranda. The slender trunk is only about 3 centimetres thick. The gently arching leaves have numerous long fine glossy dark green leaflets which droop attractively. Will grow in a wide range of climates in a frost-free shaded position.

Normanbya normanbyi: A native of the lowland rainforests north of the Daintree River in northern Queensland. Sometimes called the Australian black palm because it develops a tall slender black trunk. The leaves have handsome broad leaflets with jagged tips. Suitable for tropical and subtropical environments. To survive in Sydney's winter months it requires glasshouse conditions but is worth the effort.

Phoenix dactylifera: The date palm (commercial date). Tall-growing slender-trunked tree with a crown of stiff pinnate leaves. Similar in appearance to the Canary Island date but does not have such a dense crown or such a thick trunk. It is quite popular in Australia as a garden tree. Can be planted out in open sun. On a commercial scale, propagation is done from suckers but seed propagation is also possible. The date is a staple food of millions in the Middle East.

The date palm prefers warm dry zones in latitudes between 15° and 25° where it usually fruits every year. In zones further away from the equator its fruiting is less dependable. While it rarely fruits in Sydney, fruiting is quite good in Brisbane. Ideally for commercial production there should be a high water table to reduce the need for irrigation. The hotter and drier the climate the better the fruit. The first crop is usually obtained six years after planting but plantations take ten or more years to bear well. Once established the date palm will stand a wide range of temperatures, even withstanding severe frosts.

Phoenix reclinata: The Senegal date palm is native to tropical Africa. It naturally forms many suckers which, if not removed, develop into a cluster of leaning trunks usually about 8 to 10 metres high, the pinnate stiff leaves all bunching together. Senegal date palms planted in groups will form an attractive shade grove, giving your garden a tropical touch. Also suitable as a patio or veranda tub plant. Shows tolerance to a few degrees of frost.

Phoenix rupicola: The cliff date originates from Sikkim, in the Himalayas in India. It looks rather like the commercial date palm but has a shorter, wider trunk and a fuller leaf crown. The long leaves are not as stiff as those of the Canary Island date. Outside it makes a fine tub plant for many years before it becomes large. It is then necessary to plant it out in the ground. Like all *Phoenix* palms it takes more sun at an early stage of growth than most other palms. The cliff date is recommended as a landscape palm and will maintain its condition well indoors for periods of several weeks. It has become more readily available in Australia in recent years.

Phoenix sylvestris: Wild date palm. Very similar in appearance and dimensions to *P. canariensis.* However, its foliage is slightly softer looking and has a bluish colour. It will grow faster than the Canary Island date but its final height is only about 10 to 15 metres. Can be used indoors as a tub plant for periods of several weeks but prefers a permanent position outdoors.

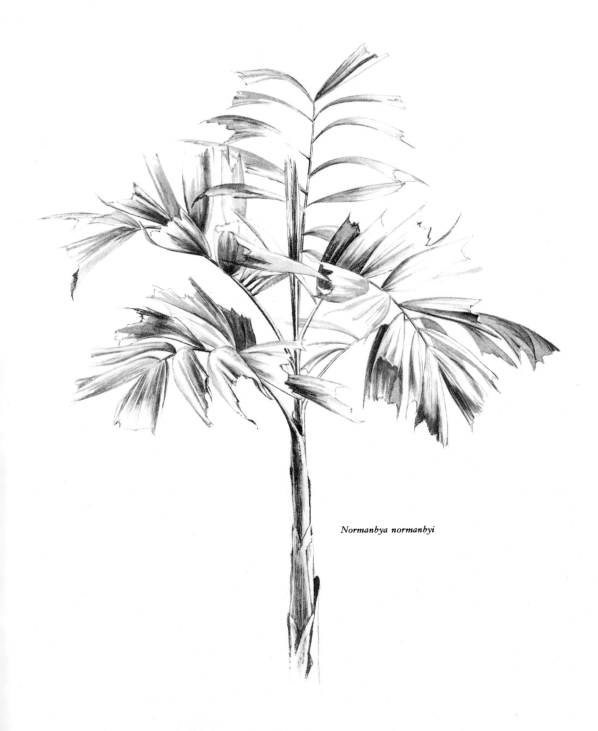

Normanbya normanbyi

Pinanga kuhlii: The Pinang palm is a tropical clustering palm from Indonesia and Malaysia. It has attractive bamboo-like trunks and wide leaflets of variable shape, the terminal ones being widest and blunt-ended. Grows to about 10 metres in the tropics. Must be grown in heated glasshouse conditions unless in the tropics. Prefers deep shade when a small plant.

Pritchardia thurstonii: A very handsome palm native to the Fiji Islands. The stiffly held fan-shaped leaves are heavily pleated and spiky in appearance. This beautiful tree will grow to 6 metres or more in the tropics and will be a dominant feature of any landscape. Needs glasshouse conditions outside the tropics.

Pritchardia pacifica: Also from the Fiji Islands, this palm is similar to *P. thurstonii* but larger.

Rheinhardtia gracilis: An extraordinarily beautiful exotic dainty palm from Mexico. It produces multiple fine stems which grow to only a metre or so. The short leaves have fine tooth-edged leaflets which are at times joined and arranged in groups along the leaf stem. At the base of the adjoining leaflets there may be "windows", a characteristic of the *Rheinhardtia* palms. Suitable as an indoor pot plant or as an outdoor plant when grown in a deeply shaded and protected site. Grows outside in Brisbane but may need a heated greenhouse for success in Sydney.

Rhopalostylis baueri: Attractive palm from Norfolk Island. The large crownshaft and upward curving leaves resemble a feather duster. Shows some cold tolerance. Suitable for pot or tub culture.

Rhopalostylis sapida: The only palm native to New Zealand, where it is called nikau or feather duster palm. Harder to grow than *R. baueri* but very hardy to cold temperatures. The leaves were used by the Maoris in roofing their huts and in making baskets and other

wares. The strongly ringed trunk grows to about 7 metres high. The flower stalk comes from below a bulbous crownshaft and after flowering produces small bright red fruit.

Roystonea regia: The royal palm or Cuban royal palm is the most common of all the *Roystonea* palms. It is not suitable for indoor culture because of its high light requirement, but it reaches majestic proportions in the garden. The trunk, which is usually enlarged at the base and slightly swollen around the middle, grows to 15 or 20 metres. Its pure elegant lines make it a good avenue tree. The long feathery leaves have rows of finely divided leaflets. Popular in tropical Australia as a garden and street tree, it also grows in temperate frost-free areas.

Sabal minor: An attractive dwarf fan-leaved palm which rarely forms a trunk. Native to Florida. It belongs to the *Sabal* group of palms otherwise called palmetto palms. Leaves are large, stiff, deeply divided and a blue-green colour. Suitable garden palm in a wide range of climates including dry inland climates.

Sabal causiarum: Grows into a giant tree with a massive trunk. The deeply divided large fan leaves are borne on long stalks.

Trithrinax acanthocoma: Native to Brazil. Its single trunk grows slowly to 3 or 4 metres. It is covered in strong sharp spines which draw a spiral pattern of thick hairy webbing. The stiffly held large dark green fan leaves form a tight crown on top of the trunk. This palm can be grown as a landscape subject in various climates since it tolerates cold well.

Veitchia joannis: A tall slender feather palm from the Fiji Islands. Leaves are arching and leaflets droop gracefully. Glossy green crownshaft under which are borne clusters of attractive red fruits 3 to 4 centimetres long. Suitable pot or garden plant in most frost-free climates.

THE PALM IMPOSTORS
9

Many plants which look like palms are botanically unrelated to them. A few actually bear the name "palm" as part of their common name and are known widely as palms. These are the most blatant of the palm impostors.

Here follows a list of some of these pseudo-palms you may meet.

Beaucarnea recurvata syn. *Nolina recurvata*: The ponytail palm or elephant foot palm. Wide spreading base which tapers towards the top into one or more slender stems crowned by reed-like drooping leaves.

Carludovicia palmata: The panama hat plant. As this name suggests, it is the source of material for the panama hat. Forms dense clumps. The fan-shaped divided leaves look indeed like palm leaves. Subtropical or tropical climates.

Cordyline australis: The New Zealand cabbage tree. Develops several stems on a sturdy base. Each stem terminates in a crown of long tapering leaves. Vary hardy to frost and to hot dry climates.

Cyathea australis: Previously *Dicksonia antarctica.* An Australian native tree fern which from time to time is referred to as a palm by the uninitiated. At first glance its long attractive fronds look like the leaves of a palm.

Cycas revoluta: The sago palm. A bushy short plant which often has several stems and thick heavy crowns of dark green palm-like fronds.

Macrozamia moorei and M. spiralis: Two common Australian native cycads which are often mistaken for palms when spotted from the roadside in their native habitat. Commonly known as pineapple palms or macrozamia palms. Their stems are usually stout and produce thick crowns of stiffly pinnate leaves. The centre of the plant produces a bright orange seed cone shaped like a pineapple.

Musa: There are thirty-five species of banana comprising the genus Musa. Many are often referred to as banana palms because of their habit of growth.

Ravenala madagascariensis: The traveller's palm. Beautiful fan-like display of leaves which are shown to best advantage if developing suckers are removed and the stem is kept single.

Xanthorrhoea: There are 15 species of Xanthorrhoea in Australia. *X. preissii* and *X. arborea* are two common species both called blackboy or blackfellow's spear because of the long spear-like spike they bear. The leaf crown looks like a rounded tuft of grass.

INDEX